Preaching the Presence of God

Preaching the Presence of God

A Homiletic from an Asian American Perspective

Eunjoo Mary Kim

Judson Press
Valley Forge

ᴅ

Preaching the Presence of God:
A Homiletic from an Asian American Perspective
© 1999 by Judson Press, Valley Forge, PA 19482-0851
All rights reserved.

Bible quotations in this volume are from the New Revised Standard Version of the Bible, copyright © 1989 by the Division of Christian Education of the National Council of the Churches of Christ in the United States of America. Used by permission. All rights reserved.

Library of Congress Cataloging-in-Publication Data

Kim, Eunjoo Mary.
    Preaching the presence of God : a homiletic from an Asian American perspective /
Eunjoo Mary Kim.
        p.   cm.
    Includes bibliographical references and index.
    ISBN 0-8170-1303-2 (pbk. : alk. paper)
    1. Preaching to Asian Americans.   I. Title.
BV4235.A83K55 1999
251'.0089'95073 – dc21   99–28021

Printed in the U.S.A.
08   07   06   05   04   03   02   01   00   99
5   4   3   2   1

OCLC# 41156519

I gratefully dedicate this book

to my husband, Seungju, and my daughter, Dorothy,

who are my everlasting supporters and dialogue partners.

Contents

Foreword

Over the last fifty years, American homiletics has experienced a revolution, both in theory and practice. A generation ago, many preaching textbooks assumed that the business of homiletics was strictly ornamental rhetoric of the most mundane sort. The serious work of biblical hermeneutics and theological analysis was to be done in some other place than the preaching classroom. Once a biblical text had been studied and exegeted, mined for its theological treasure — then and only then did the homiletician come on the scene to provide sage practical advice about such afterthoughts as form, structure, arrangement, and delivery.

Since the more dynamic ingredients in the sermon — exegesis and theological reflection — were separated from the task of sermon construction, homiletics inevitably became abstracted from both its theological and its communicational contexts. The idea that the form and language of sermons could be created apart from an act of interpretation also led inevitably to the notion that the sermon could be abstracted from its social context and from the contexts and identities of the listeners.

The last five decades of homiletical literature have formed a challenge to these views. Sermons are no longer seen as inert containers into which to pour previously determined content. Moreover, the listening environment is now understood to be bristling with variables, created by local circumstances and by such factors as ethnicity, cultural forces, and individual personalities.

Into this new wave of homiletical insight comes a remarkable book by Eunjoo Mary Kim. Over against any notion of homiletical theory created in a cultural vacuum, Kim focuses with precision and insight on the Asian American context, showing how Asian American Christians are affected by the delicate interplay between the traditional religious heritage of the East and the new cultural situation in

America. Deftly employing a variety of methods and disciplines, she does a cross-cultural analysis of Asian American congregational life and develops a homiletical practice tailored specifically to this context. In contrast to the homiletical strategies of a previous day, her approach brings together the separate flames of rhetoric, hermeneutics, theological reflection, and cultural analysis to forge the Asian American sermon.

Particularly noteworthy in this book is the way that spirituality — a crucial category in Asian religion — becomes a guiding force, summoning forth "spiritual sermons." Such preaching springs from meditative styles of exegesis and are expressed through dynamic, spiral-shaped forms. A superb model sermon, included in the last chapter, brings home the wisdom of this volume in a clear and practical way.

Eunjoo Mary Kim has given us a fine book on Asian American preaching. But she has also done much more. She has demonstrated, through her adroit use of the dialogical method and her diligent attention to the complexities of a specific cultural context, how contemporary homiletical theory should be created in any given context. The Asian American pulpit will be richer for her efforts, and the field of homiletics will be wiser for her vision.

THOMAS G. LONG

Acknowledgments

I would like to express my sincere appreciation to those who supported me in completing this work. First of all, I gratefully acknowledge three of my teachers at Princeton Theological Seminary: Thomas Long, James Kay, and Leonora Tisdale, who challenged me to rethink homiletics from the point of view of my ethnic spiritual heritage and encouraged me to give voice to that Asian American perspective. I am deeply appreciative of the generosity of the Iliff School of Theology, which gave me time to complete this book by postponing my contract. Beverly Leach's diligent proofreading helped me to communicate my thoughts and feelings in English, and her encouraging words were of great help during the writing period. I treasure the friendship and professional expertise of Alyce McKenzie who enriched the book through her meticulous reading of the manuscript. My colleague Thomas Troeger at Iliff made the book almost perfect by his thoughtful comments. I also give special thanks to Jana Childers, Thomas Long, Inn Yang, and Paul Huh for providing recommendations for the book proposal to Judson Press, and to Randy Frame, Victoria McGoey, Mary Nicol, Linda Triemstra, Rebecca Irwin Diehl, Christina Edginton, and everyone else at Judson Press who has been helpful from the beginning to the final production of this book. Finally, I wish to express my respect and gratitude for all those who stimulated me by expressing their interest and concern for the spiritual growth of Asian American communities in books and sermons.

Introduction

Homiletics is concerned with the critical and constructive thinking necessary to develop the content and method of preaching. Its history reveals that Christian preaching has always been influenced by Western rhetoric and communication theories. Since the early church, Greco-Roman rhetoric — whose main concern was to explain both how the truth might be revealed and how to speak and persuade the audience to that truth — has been the primary tool for training preachers. In *On Christian Doctrine*, Augustine, who was a teacher of rhetoric before his conversion, introduced a homiletical theory based on Ciceronian rhetoric.[1] While medieval monasticism and speculative scholarship deemphasized eloquent speech in preaching and reduced homiletical works to the collection and translation of the early church fathers' sermons,[2] interest in classical rhetoric was revived during the Reformation era. John Calvin and other Reformers who were trained under humanist teachers demonstrated their eloquence in their own sermons and commentaries. In the eighteenth and throughout the nineteenth centuries, Alexander Vinet, John Broadus, Phillips Brooks, and others understood preaching in common as a branch of rhetoric based on Aristotelian rhetorical theory and focused on instructing preachers about how to speak. The goal of speaking, in their view, was to persuade the listeners.[3]

Karl Barth and other twentieth-century theologians deemphasized rhetorical training for preachers, claiming that preaching is the proclamation of divine revelation from God's side rather than the human side.[4] However, their negative reaction to rhetoric could not dominate homiletics for long. Particularly in North America, their efforts did not succeed in separating preaching from secular rhetoric. More precisely speaking, H. Grady Davis reemphasized the significance of rhetorical elements in preaching, and his *Design for Preaching* became a landmark of contemporary North American homiletics.[5] Such contemporary homileticians as Fred Craddock, David Buttrick, and

1

Eugene Lowry have developed Davis's rhetorical notions by either extending or transforming them. In fact, their rhetorical perspective reversed the position of classical rhetoric. That is, through the influence of recent studies of theology and other human sciences and communication theories, their rhetorical concerns have moved radically from being speaker oriented to listener oriented. For them, the primary question is To whom does the preacher speak? or How does the congregation listen? rather than How should the preacher speak? Craddock's inductive movement, Buttrick's phenomenological approach to the listener's consciousness, and Lowry's narrative plot suggest that homiletics is concerned with the hearer's listening process, mode of thinking, and communication pattern.[6]

In my view, this listener-oriented perspective should be stretched to include an awareness of the ethnic diversity of the listeners and deepened to embrace culturally different communicational methods. If homiletics aims to develop a method of listener-oriented preaching, it cannot be based exclusively on the Euro-American congregation's experience and Western rhetorical theories. Instead, North American homiletics must extend itself to include the interests and concerns of non-Western congregations. After all, contemporary North American society is multiracial and multicultural, and the churches are challenged to preach God's truth in this postmodern, multicultural climate. Just as preaching takes place before diverse ethnic groups, so homiletics should be engaged with the diverse cultural and ethnic contexts of all the listeners. Homiletics must embrace the distinctiveness as well as the commonalties of different ethnic groups of listeners.

Every year Asian American churches are increasing as rapidly as are the Asian immigrant communities in general in the United States. Asian American churches have been playing an impressive role in leading their immigrant communities. Clearly they are in need of a set of homiletical theories that reflect the distinct cultural and spiritual experience of Asian American listeners. Asian American congregations have different life experiences in American society from those in their home countries. They live within the boundary of their distinctive ethnic subculture influenced by indigenous religions such as Confucian moralism and Buddhist spirituality. At the same time, they are exposed to and influenced by such general American cultural elements as democracy, capitalism, individualism, feminism, racism, and cultural colonialism. Whether they are consciously or unconsciously in the process of Americanization, they still retain their cultural DNA. It is characterized by communalism, filial piety, interdependency, and a holistic worldview, including particular ways of communicating and modes of thinking. These cultural elements not only abide in first-generation immigrants but also extend to the third and even the fourth generations. In spite of "their high level of acculturation and the intermeshing of most aspects of their lives into American society," explains Japanese American Kaoru Kendis,

> high ethnic Japanese Americans find significant differences between their own ways of interaction and those of the larger society. These differences are not the readily observable cultural elements of language, food, or dress but the more subtle, and deeply rooted values, attitudes, and behavior patterns [that] result in particular forms of interpersonal relations.... To the outsider, these differences may seem insignificant, but they constitute the primary reason high ethnic Japanese Americans have for partitioning the social segment of their lives and limiting access to it almost solely to other Japanese Americans. The instrumental aspects of their lives — making a living, getting an education, taking part in the political system — are intermeshed with mainstream society. They choose, however, to act out the more personally meaningful and satisfying noninstrumental portions of their lives with other Japanese Americans.[7]

For them, familial values, behavioral influence, and structural relationships are becoming more, rather than less, prominent as a source for identification and communication. As an example, Asian Canadian Roland Kawano says that

> Western culture teaches me to make decisions as an individual, focusing on what would result in the best interests for me, the individual. Yet, through the years I have become aware of a secondary, underlying process that is also taking place. I have come to recognize that I intuitively check in with a network of internal images that represents parents, siblings, children, significant friends, etc. The decisions I make are made thus by checking in with this significant network of relationships.[8]

In this manner, Asian Americans have experienced cultural conflict between East and West and have continued to struggle to define their distinctive ethnic roots and cultural identity as a minority group in Eurocentric American society.

Given this condition, preachers to Asian Americans are challenged to create a new homiletical approach appealing to their congregations who are situated in distinctive sociocultural contexts. The preachers feel that the homiletical theories they learned in preaching courses at seminaries do not work well for Asian American listeners. According to their preaching experiences, the European American preaching style, which emphasizes the intellectual and rational approach, or African American preaching, which stresses emotions, does not suit Asian American congregations because of this group's distinctive cultural ethos and communicational patterns. A second-generation Chinese pastor, Kenneth Uyeda Fong, born and reared in the United States and ministering in a Chinese American church in California, says about his preaching experience:

> Having just graduated from seminary at the end of 1980, I too had emerged thinking that we had all been the recipients of ministerial methods that were culturally mobile. As I embarked on my first year as a full-time pastor, I conscientiously constructed and delivered my monthly sermons as if my homiletics professors were anchored in the pews. But the premise of the IWA survey shocked my system with the potentiality of an altered reality: there might be superior ways to preach to Asian Americans about which my otherwise learned professors were either quite ignorant or unsuspecting. But what might they be?...Is there a style of preaching that would work best with Asian Americans...?[9]

The demand for an Asian American homiletic is crucial. However, there are few useful homiletical resources available for Asian American congregations. Based on my cross-cultural knowledge and preaching experience, including theological studies and the practice of the church ministry in both East and West, I propose a new preaching paradigm that is theologically and methodologically relevant to Asian American congregations. It is respectful of their particular sociocultural and spiritual experiences. I invite all theologians and preachers who are interested in the Asian American community of faith to engage in a serious and productive conversation about an Asian American homiletic. Therefore, the homiletical model I suggest is not the model but a model as a conversation starter for the Asian American homiletic. Since the search for a new paradigm for Asian American preaching is the constant theological task of all Asian American preachers, it should be a continuing process because the Asian American community of faith must be, like every faith community in the church universal, *ecclesia reformata reformanda*.

The new preaching paradigm that emerges from this book will not be limited to Asian American preaching. Rather, it extends and enriches all homiletical studies. This is because the homiletical insights and ideas discussed in this book suggest a continuing dialogue with homiletics in general and contribute to diversity in the field of homiletics. When we remember that homiletics has been developed in association with Western rhetoric and that those Western homiletical theories have dominated Christian preaching, ignoring cultural and ethnic backgrounds of the listeners, this project will participate in dismantling the imperialism of Western homiletics.

This work is a product based on the contextual method in the following respects. First, the theological premise of the entire book is God's accommodation in revelation in the Trinitarian form. God does not speak uniformly to all circumstances but accommodates according to various situations and capacities of human comprehension.[10] In order to communicate effectively with human beings, God condescends, humbles, and accommodates God's self to human categories of thought, experience, and speech.

Asian and Asian American communities confess that the Trinitarian God had been present among them and in their culture even before Western missionaries introduced Christianity to them. This means that their religious experience within the indigenous culture established the theological basis for understanding the God of Christianity, which then was reinterpreted from a Christian theological perspective. Christ is already in their culture through the Spirit and is working to transform that culture. In this sense, the context for preaching is not merely an informative resource for preaching but is the concrete locus where the preacher finds the presence and work of God the Spirit. Therefore, the homiletical ideas proposed in this book help the preacher discern God's salvific activity in the midst of congregational life. This discernment comes in light of the biblical story of the incarnated God as the foretaste of God's eschatological promise, the source of our joy in our present reality.

Second, this book is the product of serious reflection on the particular context for Asian American preaching. It begins with an analysis of the Asian American congregation, culturally, religiously, and sociopolitically, and develops homiletical insights and ideas based on that study. Christian preaching has been understood historically as the Word of God for a particular community of faith and presupposes a particular context for the preacher and congregation. An Asian American homiletic is primarily to the Asian American church for the Asian American church. It is my conviction that the universality of preaching is paradoxically present in particularity.

Here it should be noted that the term *Asian* used in this book is limited to the three East Asian countries: China, Korea, and Japan. There are cultural, religious, ethnic, and geographical variations among Asian American immigrants. Still these three geographically adjacent groups all show signs of the common influence of Confucianism, Buddhism, and shamanism. An analysis of their cultural and religious heritage and tradition will raise homiletical implications for the development of an Asian American homiletic.

The third aspect of the contextual method is that this project employs interdisciplinary dialogue with human sciences, cross-cultural studies, and other theological disciplines in order to explore the Asian American context and create a new preaching paradigm. Calvin confirms its significance in his *Institutes of the Christian Religion* saying that "Without knowledge of self there is no knowledge of God. Nearly all the wisdom we possess, that is to say, true and sound wisdom consists of two parts; the knowledge of God and ourselves."[11] Dialogue with such disciplines as anthropology, sociology, linguistics, literature, and psychology helps not only to gain full knowledge of the Word but also to deepen the understanding of divine-human communication. In addition, cross-cultural dialogue with Asian rhetoric focusing on Buddhism and Confucianism reveals that while there exists some commonality between the Asian and Western perspectives, there is considerable diversity between them. An Asian American homiletic in a current cultural context evolves by exploring those differences in some detail. Furthermore, Asian American homiletics associates with other theological disciplines. As Friedrich Schleiermacher calls practical theology "the crown of theological study,"[12] so Asian American homiletics as a subdiscipline of practical theology employs all parts of the theological enterprise, including systematic theology, biblical theology, and church history as well as pastoral theology and Christian education. All these disciplines contribute to a common goal and vision for the future of the community and enrich our theological reflection. These theological branches are interlocked and interdependent as they help Asian American homiletics seek new insights into theology and method for preaching.

Last, the approach of this project is contextual in the sense that the methodological pattern for creating a new preaching paradigm from the Asian American perspective is both dialogical and dialectical. In other words, while the traditional dialectical mode aims to create a synthesis that transcends the differences of A and B, the dialogically dialectical mode attempts to create an interdependent model based on the recognition of and respect for differences and similarities between A and B through continuing dialogue. The result is a model that neither imposes Western notions of homiletics upon the Asian American experience nor simply replaces Western-based homiletical ideas with the distinctive characteristics of Asianness. In this paradigm, Western homiletics and the Asian American perspectives are interrelated, without diminishing either one. The emphasis is on their dynamic meeting in which they challenge each other to reinterpret their concepts and to transform them to create a new set of homiletical theories. This method is possible only by an awareness that our knowledge and experience are incomplete and imperfect and that our openness to different ideas and ways of thinking is the key to the development of contemporary homiletics.

This book consists of six chapters. Chapter 1 is concerned with understanding the context for Asian American preaching. It first explores how to analyze the contemporary condition of Asian American communities and then exegetes their internal and external conditions. Their internal conditions show the influences of traditional shamanism, Confucianism, and Buddhism. The external conditions reflect present realities of racism, economic injustice, and cultural imperialism in North American society. The analysis in this initial chapter reveals that the Asian American congregation is spiritually thirsty. They need and expect sermons to be avenues through which they experience the presence and power of God the Spirit in their daily lives. They yearn to be empowered to cope with their present predicaments as a minority group in the United States and to be given spiritual direction for their personal and communal lives through preaching.

Chapter 2, as a response to the spiritual need of the listeners, explores spirituality from both Asian and Christian perspectives. Building on this discussion, it develops a theology of Asian American preaching whose focus is the nature and function of preaching and the image of the preacher. East Asian spirituality, based on the distinctive Asian religious character and cultural ethos, and Western spirituality, based on traditional Christian practice, are challenged to expand their concepts of spirituality from the perspective of Christian apocalyptic eschatology. Asian American Christian spirituality, whose foundation is the future-oriented hope in Christ Jesus, understands the spiritual journey to be proleptic, wherein the presence and work of the Holy Spirit exist as the life-giving energy of the present life of the listeners and where the community of faith functions as the locus of nurturing that spirituality. This chapter proposes spiritual preaching as a theological model for Asian American preaching. Spiritual preaching redefines both the nature and function of preaching and the image of the preacher.

Chapter 3 focuses on both an understanding of the authority of the biblical text for preaching and its interpretive method. Through examining Confucian and Buddhist hermeneutics and applying their hermeneutical implications to homiletics by means of critical conversation with various Christian hermeneutical approaches, this chapter proposes spiritual hermeneutics. While contemporary hermeneutical theories emphasize the preacher's imagination and intellectual approach to the text, spiritual hermeneutics goes further, stressing the significance of intuitive meditation for biblical interpretation. The various practices of intuitive meditation in Buddhism and Confucianism and the rediscovery of the significance of the practice of an ancient Christian meditative reading of *lectio divina* give insights into the development of spiritual hermeneutics. This interpretive method aims to produce new meaning from the text by meditation and allows the text to function in preaching as an eschatological parable or paradigm through which the congregation experiences the spiritual presence of God.

Chapter 4 gives attention to the design of a spiritual sermon. Agreeing with the contemporary homiletical view that the sermonic form should correspond to the listeners' epistemological process, this chapter analyzes the characteristics of Asian ways of communicating and attempts to have a dialogue with Western homiletical theories. Homiletical implications derived from such Asian ways of communicating as holistic knowing, the pursuit of consensus, the dialogue of silence, and indirect communication have implications for the development of a spiral-form sermon that employs the listeners' intuition as the divine communicational channel. The spiral-form sermon designed as a space-oriented movement gives the listeners a meditative moment in which they experience intuitive enlightenment or "the shock of recognition"[13] under the guidance of the Holy Spirit.

Chapter 5 concentrates on language for spiritual preaching. Considering that most homiletical concepts about language are heavily dependent on Western rhetorical tradition and that most preachers have been trained in Western rhetoric at seminaries, unaware of the significance of Asian rhetoric for preaching, this chapter attempts to develop a new concept and use of language for spiritual preaching from the perspective of Asian rhetoric. The examination of Confucian and Buddhist rhetoric reemphasizes the significance of poetic and metaphorical language in preaching and reveals that preaching as religious discourse should be conversational. This chapter gives insights into the development of the language of conversation for preaching by paying attention to the language used in writing a private letter.

The last chapter offers an example of spiritual preaching. Using my own sermon preached at a Korean American church where I served as pastor, this chapter attempts to show how the homiletical insights developed in the earlier chapters can be put into the practice of preaching. The sample sermon is analyzed and explained in order to help the reader gain a sense of how the preceding discussion about the exegesis of the congregation, the theology of preaching, the interpretation of the text, the design of the sermon, and the use of language can be incorporated into one sermon. This sermon is not presented as an absolute model of spiritual preaching but is offered as an example by which the reader is encouraged to practice spiritual preaching in his or her ministry of preaching.

Notes

1. Augustine, *On Christian Doctrine,* vol. 4, trans. D. W. Robertson Jr. (New York: Macmillan, 1958).
2. Paul Scott Wilson, *A Concise History of Preaching* (Nashville: Abingdon, 1992), 67–72.
3. See Alexander Vinet, *Homiletics* (New York: Visions & Phinney, 1855); Phillips Brooks, *On Preaching* (New York: Seabury 1964); John Broadus, *On the Preparation and Delivery of Sermons,* rev. Vernon L. Standfield (San Francisco: Harper, 1979).
4. See Karl Barth, *Homiletics* (Louisville: Westminster/John Knox, 1991); John Knox, *The Integrity of Preaching* (New York: Abingdon, 1957).
5. H. Grady Davis, *Design for Preaching* (Philadelphia: Muhlenberg, 1958).
6. See Fred Craddock, *As One Without Authority* (Nashville: Abingdon, 1971); *Preaching* (Nashville: Abingdon, 1987); David Buttrick, *Homiletic: Moves and Structures* (Philadelphia: Fortress, 1987); Eugene L. Lowry, *The Homiletical Plot: The Sermon As Narrative Art Form* (Atlanta: John Knox, 1978); *How to Preach a Parable: Designs for Narrative Sermons* (Nashville: Abingdon, 1989).
7. Kaoru Oguri Kendis, *A Matter of Comfort: Ethnic Maintenance and Ethnic Style Among Third-Generation Japanese Americans* (New York: AMS Press, 1989), 6, quoted from V. B. Y. Choy, "Decision Making and Conflict in the Congregation," in *People on the Way: Asian North Americans Discovering Christ, Culture, and Community,* ed. David Ng (Valley Forge, Pa.: Judson, 1996), 252–53.
8. Roland Kawano, "Reflections on Asian Canadian Search for Identity," in *PAACCE Ministries* 9, no. 2 (August 1993): 1, quoted from Choy, 255.
9. Kenneth Uyeda Fong, *Insights for Growing Asian-American Ministries* (Rosemead, Calif.: Evergrowing Publications, 1990), 116–17.
10. David Willis, "Rhetoric and Responsibility in Calvin's Theology," in *The Context of Contemporary Theology: Essays in Honor of Paul Lehmann,* ed. Alexander J. McKelway and David Willis (Atlanta: John Knox, 1974), 53.
11. John Calvin, *Institutes of the Christian Religion,* trans. Ford Lewis Battles (Philadelphia: Westminster, 1987), 1.1.1.
12. Friedrich Schleiermacher, *Christian Caring: Selections from Practical Theology* (Philadelphia: Fortress, 1988), 99.
13. Craddock, 145.

Chapter One

The Congregation

Christian preaching, as a form of public communication, presupposes a group of listeners. The preacher prepares a sermon for a particular group at one particular time and place and delivers it to them as the Word of God. The corporate group of listeners is the congregation, the people of faith, the church, where the individual members share their beliefs and organize to do God's will in the circumstances of their lives. Preaching is carefully aimed toward a particular group of listeners, the congregation. Just as individual Christians are unknown in Scripture apart from a community of faith, so individual listeners in preaching cannot be considered separate from the congregation.[1]

Understanding the Congregation

An Asian American homiletic begins by understanding the congregation as a corporate group of listeners. The congregation never hear the Word of God in an abstract setting or apart from the realities of their own social and personal lives. Their needs are related to issues of the society to which they belong; personal concerns are related to regional, national, and global issues and problems. Therefore, as James F. Hopewell describes, "No congregation is a 'pure gospel' church, composed solely of inarguably Christian practices; no living church escapes the contribution that a wider culture makes to its nature and continuing history."[2]

The congregation is an active contributor to the sermon in three ways. First, in the pastor's preparation to preach, the congregation functions like a homiletical treasury in which the preacher can gain theological and methodological insights into and implications for the proclamation of the Word of God. The life experience and faith journey of the congregation are rich context-specific resources for preaching. Christ has been present in the circumstances of the congregation before the sermon is formalized, and the congregation preserves particular memories of what God has done and how faithful responses have been made by them to God's action. The subculture of the congregation conveys stories, rituals, customs, idioms, and symbols within the particular community of faith, and knowledge about them helps the preacher turn the sermon into a profound dialogue with the congregation. The preacher has the privilege of wrestling with the theological and existential issues raised by the congregation's experiences. The preacher learns how to describe God's grace in preaching both from and to the localized expressions of their beliefs and experiences.

Second, the congregation participate in the practice of preaching as ongoing dialogue partners. They are not passive but active in responding to the sermon as a group, sharing common experiences in the past and present and having a common goal for the future in the promise of God. In their modes of thinking they expect to be challenged by preaching and motivated for renewal in their actions. While listening to the sermon, they bring to the hearing their personal, spiritual, and social experiences and participate in the preaching by thinking, feeling, and deciding. Thomas G. Long puts it this way:

> The hearer is not at all passive in the listening process. The space between pulpit and pew bristles with energy and activity. As the preacher speaks, the hearer races ahead in anticipation of what might be said next, ranges back over what has already been said, debates with the preacher, rearranges the material, adds to the message, wanders away and returns (sometimes!). In short, the hearer is a co-creator of the sermon. Preachers may be passing out eggs, but hearers are making omelets, and a sermon preached to seventy-five people is actually transformed by them into seventy-five more-or-less-related sermons.[3]

Finally, the congregation are the agents for fulfilling preaching. They are not a static but a dynamic group of believers who live with and for the Word. They desire to transform their community by the Word of God into an alternative community in the midst of the prevailing secular cultural setting. So, preaching does not end in a limited, finite place and time in a worshiping context. Rather, preaching is an ongoing event that has to be fulfilled within the daily life of the listeners. To such contexts as the lives of factory workers, social workers, doctors, lawyers, teachers, policemen, farmers, businessmen, and housekeepers, the congregation carry the Word and are charged to live by and for it. Likewise, the congregation make the preached Word of God become flesh and dwell in the world. Its members are a bridge connecting the Word of God proclaimed in a liturgical context to the larger context of society. Therefore, the goal of preaching is accomplished not by the preacher at the preaching moment but by the congregation after the moment of preaching.

Whereas sufficient knowledge of the congregation is the prerequisite for the preparation and practice of effective preaching, it is not simple to describe the Asian American congregation in general. This is because there are no homogeneous congregations, either in terms of the stage of faith development or in terms of age, gender, education, occupation, or personal experience. Moreover, individual local congregations have their own particular issues and problems due to the geographical location of the church, theological trends of the congregation, and the characteristics of the leadership of the church.

While acknowledging the particular character of each local congregation, this chapter attempts to help the preacher understand the "corporate personality"[4] of the Asian American congregation through analyzing and exploring the characteristics they often share. Just as a person is not an isolated unit but part of a whole to which he or she belongs, so the diverse individual members of the congregation interact with one another at a group level and create a rich and complex group identity. The corporate personality of the group is formed by the distinctive ethnic tradition and language of the congregation, its faith history, the geographical location and size of the church, the social class and economic status of the members, and the sociopolitical structure of the larger society to which the congregation belongs. This subculture of the congregation influences the formation of the identity and lifestyle of the individual members and is expressed implicitly and explicitly in all such forms of ecclesial activity as worship, Bible study, prayer meetings, church organizations, administrative meetings, and mission programs.

Asian American congregations share characteristics of corporate personality with one another because they are rooted in common Asian cultural backgrounds and common experiences as ethnic minorities in the United States. Their commonality can be explained internally and externally. Internally, each group shares a cultural ethos formulated by the same religious heritage and by its geographical proximity to one another. The cultural elements of such indigenous religions as Confucianism, Buddhism, and shamanism have influenced the formation of a distinctive East Asian ethos not only in a religious sense but also in the whole way of Asian lifestyle, including worldviews, a set of values, customs, and traditions. Externally, as an ethnic minority group, they face common problems arising from the sociopolitical strata of American society. Historicopolitical and socioeconomic analyses of the congregation reveal urgent problems within the community and awaken the preacher to deal with them seriously in preaching. These two internal and external conditions have been interwoven and have contributed to the formation of the distinctive corporate personality of the Asian American congregation.

How, then, can the preacher become aware of this distinctive character? Knowledge of the internal and external conditions of the congregation can be gained by cross-cultural dialogue and interdisciplinary studies. In addition to formal studies about Asian religions and culture, appreciation for Asian American literature, drama, painting, sculpture, and music help reveal how Asian Americans feel and experience life. Moreover, reading books and journals related to minority groups in the United States or such activities as listening to the personal experiences of Asian Americans, visiting Asian American institutions, and interviewing their community leaders are helpful resources for understanding the Asian American community. Furthermore, the preacher's pastoral sensitivity and realistic imagination are important tools for understanding the context for Asian American preaching because through these the preacher shares the experiences and problems of the congregation directly or indirectly.

The internal and external conditions of the Asian American congregation that are explored by means of such methods are summarized below.

Internal Conditions

Most Asian Americans are familiar with traditional Asianness. They are the bearers of Asian tradition and culture because they have a relatively short immigrant history compared with that of other ethnic immigrant groups. Large-scale immigration followed the 1965 Immigration and Naturalization Act. In the case of Korean Americans, more than 75 percent are first-generation immigrants, more than 80 percent of whom arrived after 1965.[5] Their first language was Korean, and their personalities and lifestyles were formed in Korea. Asian American churches are mostly composed of these first-generation Asians. They preserve traditional Asianness and pass it on to the next generation. The members bring to the church many enculturated religious elements of Christian faith and contribute to the formation of its subculture.

While there are many determining elements in the subcultures of Asian American congregations, their cultural ethos and religious practices have been influenced mostly by three East Asian religions: Confucianism, Buddhism, and shamanism.[6] These traditional religions have co-existed in China, Korea, and Japan for thousands of years and have influenced various aspects of the Asian way of life personally and communally. They have contributed positively or negatively to producing distinctive Asian characteristics not only in religious life but also in overall lifestyle. They have also influenced in certain ways the formation of the Christian faith. Symbols, ritual practices, and doctrinal and ideological instructions of Christianity have been syncretized visibly and invisibly with the elements of these traditional religions, and this enculturation has contributed to the creation of particularities of Christian faith in East Asia. Therefore, it is not an overstatement to say that Asian American culture is based on the syncretization of these three religions and that the internal conditions of Asian American churches have been influenced by them.

The following exploration of Confucianism, Buddhism, and shamanism will help the preacher realize the impact of these three religions on the formation of the corporate personality of the Asian American congregation.

The Influence of Confucianism in East Asia

Confucianism originates in the teachings of Confucius and his disciples. Confucius (551–479 B.C.) was born in the feudal society of the Chou dynasty (1111–249 B.C.). Without benefit of a regular teacher, he managed to become a mature learned man and served the state as a high-ranking government officer. Feeling disappointed by an unjust sociopolitical reality, he resigned his position and traveled around the state consulting rulers and teaching his pupils. After his death, his teachings were compiled by his pupils in the *Analects, Great Learning*, and the *Doctrine of the Mean*.

Although most Confucian teaching is combined with traditional Chinese humanitarian thought and concepts, the idea of the perfect man is distinctively attributed to Confucius. According to Confucius, the perfect man means the morally perfect man, that is, the superior man. He is a man of "earnestness, liberality, truthfulness, diligence, and generosity. He is respectful in private life, serious in handling affairs, and loyal in dealing with others. He studies extensively, is steady in his purpose, inquires earnestly, and reflects on things at hand. In short, he is a man of all virtues."[7]

These qualities are gained through self-discipline and are practiced in five categories of human relationships: king-subject, parent-child, husband-wife, older brother-younger brother, friend with friend. These five categories are based on reciprocal responsibility; that is, benevolence in rulers and loyalty from subjects; kindness from parents and filial piety from children; righteous behavior from the husband and obedience from the wife; gentility in the elder sibling and humility in the younger; and faithfulness and trust among friends. However, these reciprocal relationships have often been misunderstood as hierarchism, placing ruler over subject, parent over child, man over woman, and elder over younger. As the original concern for mutual responsibility in the unity and harmony of these relationships was lost, the five categories became instead the ideological foundation for a hierarchical Asian society.

Confucianism has been practiced not only as sociopolitical and personal moral principles and precepts but also as a religious faith in at least two ways. One is that the ultimate goal of Confucian teachings is to direct people to sagehood. The other is that Confucian rituals are based on imposing religious meaning on a reverence for one's ancestors. This suggests that of the five relationships in Confucian ideology, the one receiving the greatest attention in practice was filial piety. The expression of this relationship extended to the worship of ancestors as a moral duty. It was believed that if one kept a good relationship with the spirits of the dead, they in turn would bless one's offspring and protect them from the disasters of this world.[8]

In China Confucianism was developed throughout the Tang and Sung dynasties. The central Confucian theme that is represented by the Five Virtues — humanity, righteousness, propriety, wisdom, and faithfulness — was strongly reasserted during the Tang dynasty (A.D. 610–910) by such Confucian scholars as Han Yu and Li Ao. Throughout the Sung dynasty (A.D. 960–1279), Neo-Confucianism became the foundation of political and educational reforms. It emphasized the study of the Confucian classics as a guide for a moral and ethical life. Its philosophy and practice were based upon the religious conviction that all humans could cultivate moral perfection by diligence, faithfulness, and loyalty.[9] In modern China, Neo-Confucian ideology was challenged by Western military imperialism and technological superiority and lost its official status. Since the Communist victory in 1949 and the Cultural Revolution in the 1960s, Marxist-Leninist ideology has replaced Confucian teachings.

In Korea Confucianism was introduced in the late fourth century A.D. In the early period of its introduction, Confucian precepts and scholarly teachings were tools for aristocratic codes of behavior and formed the foundation of the state's educational system. During the Yi dynasty (A.D. 1392–1910), Neo-Confucianism achieved status as a dominant state ideology. The state ran a comprehensive school system and taught Confucian texts, such as the Four Books and Five Classics, and various Chinese works of poetry and history. These writings were the main texts in the civil service examination and were included in the curriculum at the Royal College and other schools. In the first period of the Yi dynasty, Confucian values and mores were only for the Yangban, a small class governing a large commoner class. However, by the end of the eighteenth century, as all classes had an opportunity for education and training, Confucian ethics and mores rapidly spread even to the lower strata of society.[10] By the time that Protestantism was introduced to Korea in the nineteenth century, Korean society was Confucianized in all aspects. However, in the face of modernization and industrialization, Koreans have questioned the relevance of Confucian moral values and principles.[11]

In Japan, according to the earliest chronicles, Confucianism was introduced near the end of the third century by the Korean scholar Wani, who brought the *Analects* to the court of Emperor Ojin. Since then, more Confucian texts were introduced to Japan through Korea, and those texts influenced the formation of government policies and administrations. During the Tokugawa period (1600–1868), Neo-Confucianism became the state ideology and penetrated the popular culture of Japan by the second half of the seventeenth century. In the 1890 Imperial Rescript on Education, Confucian principles and values of loyalty, duty, and filial piety were introduced into the standard curriculum, and later these principles contributed to the formation of Japanese nationalism. They served to justify Japanese imperialist invasions in Korea, in Manchuria, and in the Japanese-controlled portions of North China during the early twentieth century. After World War II, Confucian teachings were removed from the Japanese curriculum. However, such Confucian virtues and ideals as "harmony and loyalty" are still fundamental to the substrata of Japanese society.[12]

It seems that Confucianism has lost favor in the sense that it is no longer the official state ideology in East Asian countries. Nonetheless, it is not an exaggeration to say that Confucian morality and ideology have greatly affected the Asian way of life. Filial piety is stressed as a means of humanity in highly modernized Asian society, and Confucian morality and self-cultivation — emphasizing hard work, diligence, and self-discipline — have helped to shape a hard-driving industrial work force in modern Asia. However, Confucianism also undergirds a patriarchal hierarchy, a social ideology that serves as a useful tool for male-centered hierarchical order in the community.

The Confucian ideologies of loyalty and obedience to authority have often been misused in the contemporary Asian context. For example, Korean military governments from the 1960s to 1980s forced the people to subordinate themselves to unjust dictatorships by emphasizing the virtue of Confucian loyalty to the king under the pretense of national solidarity. In modern Japan, there was an effort to restore Confucian morality as the principle of public education in order to fill the moral void of modern society. Such attempts have prevented modern Asia from establishing an egalitarian democratic society, since in the Confucian hierarchical system of patriarchy, the position of women and children becomes weakened, while patriarchal authority is strengthened.

The Influence of Confucianism on Asian American Churches

The Confucian tradition is also deeply rooted in Asian American churches in many respects. First, churches affirm the Confucian values of self-cultivation, emphasizing education, hard work, honesty, perseverance, and diligence. Lives are morally conservative and family centered.[13] These Confucian values characterize not only first-generation immigrants but also their offspring. They have been passed down through family education and interaction within the Asian American community.[14]

Asian American congregations have frequent meetings for worship, fellowship, and Bible study and help one another build a community based on Christian love. For example, most Korean American churches have Sunday morning and evening worship services, a Wednesday service, a Friday Bible study meeting, seasonal revival meetings, and regular early morning prayer meetings. Pastors regularly preach seven to nine times a week. Such ecclesial practices are rooted in the tradition of the church in Korea, where most Korean American pastors had their ministerial backgrounds. About half (51.3 percent) of all church members were previously affiliated with churches in Korea.[15] Naturally, then, a Korean style of religious practice maintains a strong hold on their churches in the United States. However, it should be noted that frequent services and meetings often lead the congregation to feel burdened by their church lives. Moreover, frequent preaching prevents the preacher from having enough time to create quality sermons.

Filial piety, a second influence of Confucianism, is an important ethical rule in both Asian American families and the church. Such values as respect, obedience, and benevolence are still maintained, based on reciprocal responsibility and interdependency. Young people care for family elders, respect them, and make them a part of their lives. Older people participate in family and community affairs as advisors with their wisdom and experience. In family life, parents want to impress strong values on children through admonition. The relationship between parents and children is stricter than that in most European American families.

In this manner, Asian American congregations are like one homogeneous racial family. Laity are expected to respect pastors and elders as if they are parents and to obey their instruction. In turn, church leaders have the responsibility to care for the laity with love and authority. In this hierarchical system, many Asian American preachers regard themselves as heralds of God who are sent by God from above. The congregation is expected to accept the words from the preacher's mouth as the Word of God and to obey the preacher's instructions humbly. The typical preaching style is the authoritative three-point deductive approach with rigid, simplistic, and humorless prescriptive and imperative language.

While such a hierarchical system has ruled the Asian and Asian American pulpit for a long time, it should be noted that when it is practiced too rigidly, it often strains the relationship between those who are above and those who are below. Congregations who live in the egalitarian and democratic idealism of American society are not happy with such a traditional Confucian view of the pulpit. Rather, they want to understand preaching from an egalitarian and reciprocal perspective. That is, they want to regard the preacher as a friend who helps and encourages them through dialogue rather than authoritative dogma. They also prefer the conversational approach in preaching over an authoritative unilateral approach, in which their daily experiences and theological questions are seriously considered and where they participate in eliciting new meaning from the biblical text. At this point, Asian American preaching is challenged to reconsider the preacher's authority and preaching style from an egalitarian perspective.

Patriarchal authority, a third influence of Confucianism, results in sexism in Asian American churches. According to Confucius, women are inherently inferior to men and incompetent to perform nondomestic activities.[16] Women are required to demonstrate modesty, obedience, conformity, and obligation. They are left out of family and church situations, where they are able neither to participate in the decision-making process nor to assume active roles using their own freedom and independent judgment. For example, although 68 percent of Korean immigrant Protestant church members are women, they are allowed to serve the church neither as elders nor as ministers in many churches.[17] The authority of the preacher is given automatically by the preacher's masculine gender. Many preachers describe the virtues of Christian women in terms of obedience, and they force subordination to male authority and leadership both at home and within the church.

It is worth noting, however, that in American society the Asian American woman's experience reveals a different kind of ideal woman. No longer confined to the domestic world, growing numbers of women are encouraged to participate outside the home. Many have had more economic freedom, opportunities for individual expression, and a sense of self-worth and self-esteem than they do in Asian Confucian society. The Confucian ideal of women is not necessarily valid for Asian American women. In this regard, the preacher's urgent theological task is to develop a gender-inclusive theological perspective and practice that can embrace women in the center of the community equally with men at both the congregational and ministerial levels.

The traditional Confucian mode of thinking based on "my family and my community" is a fourth influence and persists in Asian American churches. Family- and kinship-oriented value systems are preserved in their organizational structure. Regardless of the length of residence, almost all Asian American churchgoers indicate their strong sense of family priority, ethnic pride, and preference for teaching their native language to their children.[18]

Contributing to the reinforcement of the Asian American community's identity are European Americans' exclusive attitudes about minority. However, this kind of social relationship could degenerate into tribalism or ethnocentrism when practiced in self-centered ways. In this regard, preachers should realize that stressing self-centered ethnic solidarity through preaching may create conflicts with other racial groups. Asian American preaching must expand the Confucian perspective for the formation of an ideal community from "my family and my community" to "our society and our human race" for harmony and unity of the world.[19]

Finally, Confucian moralism is embedded deeply in the content and style of Asian American preaching. Much sermonic content is concerned with moral exhortations for the Christian life. It is based on the literal knowledge of the Bible and delivered through legalistic and prescriptive language. Such a moralistic approach, however, does not appeal to contemporary Asian American congregations, particularly to second-generation listeners who have been educated in American schools. Rather, these American-educated listeners challenge the preacher to develop a Christian theological perspective by which they can test and establish their ethnic values and guidelines. They want preaching to be heard in an egalitarian way through descriptive and indicative language rather than authoritative, judgmental language.

This emerging new situation of the Asian American church requires preachers to take seriously the changing mentality of their congregations. People in general resist shifting paradigms; so do preachers. However, while maintaining traditional outlooks and approaches to the preaching ministry brings a certain stability and security to preachers, sustaining the Confucian hierarchism in the preaching ministry can be a stumbling block that causes serious divisions within the church. In this context, Asian American preaching is challenged to reform its content and homiletical methods.

The Influence of Buddhism in East Asia

Buddhism is defined in general as a religion created in India around the fourth or fifth century B.C. by a religious group that followed the teaching and practice of the Buddha. It has grown as a pan-Asian religious tradition whose characteristics differ according to the surrounding culture. Gautama, the Buddha, was born about 536 B.C. in the Himalayan foothills of India. Through his spiritual journey seeking release from life's suffering and problems, he experienced enlightenment (the awakening of the truth) and devoted the rest of his life to preaching and teaching his doctrine. The essence of this effort is represented in the Four Noble Truths that the Buddha grasped through enlightenment: all life is suffering; the cause of suffering is desire; stopping desire will stop suffering; and the Eightfold Path is the best way to stop desire. The Eightfold Path, which includes the right views, right intention, right speech, right action, right livelihood, right effort, right mindfulness, and right concentration, is the way to reach *nirvana*.[20] In this manner, Buddhist teaching is related to the ideas of nonself, emptiness, and enlightenment through insight.

After the death of the Buddha, his disciples began to collect and disseminate his teachings, and Buddhism became a missionary religion. New schools and movements evolved steadily, including a great variety of scholarly treatises and monastic rules that claimed to be part of the Buddha's original message. The two mainline schools were Mahayana (the Great Vehicle) and Hinayana (the Small Vehicle). While Hinayana schools produced anthropomorphic images of the Buddha with sophisticated artistic expressions and salvation limited exclusively to a small group of disciplined monks,[21] Mahayana schools emphasized that everyone could attain enlightenment or "become Buddha" by means of Buddha's compassion and resourcefulness in saving all living creatures. For them, to pursue one's own salvation apart from that of other living beings seemed selfish. The full saint would remain in the world in order to help save other living beings. This openness to the laity's spiritual needs and salvation encouraged an idea of the *bodhisattva*, which became one of the central doctrines of Mahayana Buddhism and the foundation of such Buddhist devotional sects as the Pure Land sect.

Bodhisattvas are beings who have attained all the qualities needed to enter the blessed state, *nirvana*, but have refrained voluntarily from entering because of their compassion for others who need and seek freedom and salvation from the suffering of this world. *Bodhisattvas* are a manifestation or an incarnation of Buddha himself. In other words, Buddha comes into the secular world to save us with compassion. *Bodhisattvas'* compassionate love and concern for the people in this world advocate the image of the ideal human being as a compassionate and sacrificial being. This ideal of *bodhisattva* is the essence of hope for liberation and salvation of the common people.

From the second century B.C. to the first century A.D., Buddhism was a powerful force throughout the Indian subcontinent, and it

spread into Central Asia and China. Mahayana Buddhism was initially introduced to China in the first century A.D. through the Silk
Road, the transcontinental caravan route, by Buddhist missionaries.
Although it was condemned in the beginning as barbarian because its
doctrine ran counter to the teachings of China's most revered sages,
Buddhism spread to all regions and social levels by the sixth century
and then enjoyed a golden age under the Tang dynasty. It became an
important factor in Chinese civilization.

Due to the geographical distance between India and China, Buddhism in China developed in its own way by assimilating itself with
such indigenous religions as Taoism and Confucianism. As a result
of creative acculturation, the meditation school, known in China as
Chan, in Korea as Sôn, and in Japan as Zen, appeared in the seventh
century as a unique blend of Taoism and the various meditative practices of Mahayana Buddhism. It appealed to intellectual circles. It is
also notable that Buddhist philosophy contributed to the development
of Neo-Confucian metaphysics and spirituality.

Since the Sung dynasty, Buddhism has lost the support of elite
groups and the upper classes because of the government's reinforcement of Confucianism. Although there were various attempts to
revive Buddhism in modern China, the Communist government on
mainland China suppressed the Buddhist faith and destroyed its temples and valuable works of art. Yet, Buddhism had been the most
popular religion among the common people of China before 1949.[22]
It was syncretized with indigenous folk religions and functioned to
express the people's religiosity. Since then, Chinese Buddhism has
moved to Taiwan, Hong Kong, and the West, especially to North
American immigrant communities in California, New York, and
Toronto, and its leaders are working to spread the knowledge of
Buddhism beyond the ethnic community.

Korea was introduced to Chinese Mahayana Buddhism in the
late fourth century and was influenced by both the Pure Land and
Zen schools.[23] Pure Land Buddhism is a prayer-offering religion. It
understands faith to be an aspiration given by the grace of *Amitabha*
Buddha, the lord of Pure Land, and stresses the sanctification of the
believers by means of good works and good thinking in order to be
reborn in the western paradise over which *Amitabha* Buddha presides.

The salvation of the believer depends on the grace of *Amitabha* Buddha, her compassion for the common people, and the mediating role of *bodhisattvas*. Zen Buddhism is a religion of self-enlightenment that advocates meditation and self-discipline. It puts great emphasis on the strenuous effort of the individual to gain enlightenment. While Pure Land Buddhism stresses the purely emotional aspects of faith, requiring wholehearted love and devotion to *Amitabha* Buddha, Zen Buddhism concentrates on the volitional and cognitive aspects of faith.[24] In Korean Buddhism, these two branches of Buddhism are practiced together so that emotional dependence and cognitive enlightenment have coherence in the journey of faith.

Although Buddhism was primarily concerned with the individual's salvation, it also functioned in the particular Korean historical context as *hoguk pulgyo* (state-protection Buddhism). That is, as Korea was frequently under the threat of foreign invasion, the Unified Silla (A.D. 668–935) and Koryo dynasty (A.D. 937–1392) used Buddhism as a centripetal force to unite the people by synthesizing its doctrine and ritual practice with the ideology of national security and peace.[25] Buddhism was officially adopted as the state religion during the Koryo dynasty, when Buddhist civilization rose to the peak of its brilliance. In the synthesis of such Buddhist soteriology and Korean religious practice, such Korean Buddhist scholars as Uichon and Chinul created a distinctive Korean Buddhist school, called the Chogyechong.

However, the subsequent corruption of Buddhist monasteries and excessive political intervention by Buddhist monks and officials resulted in their severe persecution by the Yi dynasty (A.D. 1392–1910), which succeeded the Koryo dynasty. Although since then Buddhism has lost its predominant political power, it has continued to play a role as a major component in Korean religion and culture. As David Kwang-sun Suh indicates, it cannot be denied that throughout its long history, Buddhism gradually acculturated in Korea by merging with indigenous shamanistic cults and ideologies until it became a religion of wish-fulfillment among the common people, losing its main ideas of nonself and emptiness.[26] It is also true that Pure Land devotionalism and the compassion of *Amitabha* Buddha have been the foundation of Korean spirituality and religious ethos.

As it was in Korea, Buddhism in Japan has been assimilated with the indigenous religions and traditions. After Korea introduced Buddhist scriptures and Buddha statues to the Japanese royal court in the middle of the sixth century, Buddhism civilized Japanese culture with its profound philosophical and religious doctrine and elaborate liturgy. Earlier, Buddhism had been known within the royal household and among influential court nobles who reinterpreted their native Shinto religion according to the Buddhist doctrine of *bodhisattvas* and borrowed Buddhist art and ritual to use in Shinto shrines.[27]

During the medieval age of the Kamakura dynasty (A.D. 1185–1333) Buddhism spread to the general population and reached its apex. Japanese monks Eisai (A.D. 1141–1214) and Dogen (A.D. 1200–1253) visited China and returned to introduce Zen Buddhism to Japan. Its temples served as the educational center for Zen doctrine and practice and other Chinese learning, including Neo-Confucianism.[28] Buddhism in Japan was peculiarly modified by the shamanistic native religion of Shinto and was syncretized to unite harmoniously with Shinto tradition. Since the Meiji restoration in 1868, which mobilized the nation under the authority of the emperor, the government gave a definite priority to Shinto, and Buddhism lost its privileged status. However, the syncretistic influence is still deeply rooted in the cultural and religious lives of the common people.

Buddhism has been the most popular religion among East Asians. Its doctrine and liturgy influenced their spiritual lives and contributed to the civilization of popular culture. Its religious characters have been deeply embedded in Asian culture and the popular mentality.

The Influence of Buddhism on Asian American Churches

Buddhism has also influenced Asian and Asian American churches to a great extent. First, Buddhist teachings have helped Asian and Asian American churches understand Christian doctrine. When Christianity was introduced to Asia by Western missionaries, much Christian doctrine paralleled Buddhist teachings in several respects. The ideal of the *bodhisattvas* was similar to Christian soteriology based on incarnation and the sacrificial love of God. The compassionate sacrifice of *bodhisattvas* became a theological resource for understanding God's personality. The concept of liberation and salvation in Mahayana

Buddhism paved the way to accepting Christian eschatology in the communal sense.

Second, the Buddhist disciplines of prayer, meditation, and the practice of love through charity have reinforced the practice of Christian discipleship. Particularly Korean Christians, who lived in the culture influenced by the Pure Land devotionalism, took seriously the regular practice of prayer, worship, and offering. Services of early morning prayer and weekday worship reflect the influence of Buddhist religious practice within Korean and Korean American churches. Moreover, giving is a popular theme of preaching because sharing possessions is considered a primary way of Christian commitment for salvation.

Third, the long-term combination of emotional Pure Land Buddhism and cognitive Zen Buddhism has formulated an Asian religious ethos that is universal and holistic. This means that Asians tend to regard religious faith as an integral unity of emotion and cognition. In the process of searching for truth, the human mind and heart will work together as inseparable, integral parts to help the individual transcend worldly matters. This kind of epistemology is also applied to preaching. For Asians, preaching is a process of searching for truth. At the moment of preaching, they want to experience holistic enlightenment. In other words, they want to be touched deeply by the sermon, emotionally as well as intellectually, so that they experience a committed transformation of themselves. Therefore, preaching that focuses merely on either an intellectual aspect or an emotional response is insufficient to satisfy the spiritual needs of the Asian American congregation.

The Influence of Shamanism

Shamanism, as Mircea Eliade defines it, is a religious phenomenon that has prevailed in Siberia, inner Asia, North and South America, Indonesia, Oceania, and elsewhere. Its basis is animism, which is the belief that every material object has animus or soul. The world is comprised of a vast number of gods, demons, and ancestral spirits responsive only to the shaman, who is able to communicate with them. Shamanism exists in China, Korea, and Japan as native folk religions with certain variations from one country to another. It has survived for thousands of years by coexisting with other religious cultural forms and contents, and it assumes distinctive characteristics according to its particular geographical historical background. Its primary concerns are the matters of this world — life, health, fertility, victory over death, disease, sterility, and disaster. East Asians have instinctively believed that these gods or spirits are morally neutral. They are benevolent and good if people maintain a good relationship with them. The spirits have power to bless them with wealth, fortune, peace, and health.

The term *shaman* (*wu* in China, *mudang* in Korea, and *miko* in Japan), derives from Tungus, an Altaic language related to Manchurian in northern China. The shaman either inherits the tradition from his or her family or comes to it independently by finding divine inspiration from spirit illness. Those who become shamans through the process of suffering spirit illness and effecting healing are more revered than are those who inherit their status.[29] Generally the shaman assumes the three roles of priest, healer, and prophet, mediating between this world and the otherworld through ecstatic experiences and soul flight. While institutionalized religions tend to be patriarchal, emphasizing the masculine in their doctrines and liturgy, shamanism includes a significant female role. Female shamans are the key figures mediating the human world and the divine by contacting spirits and ancestral souls through ecstasy.

Throughout the history of Chinese religion, shamanism has been with the people as their primitive native religion since ancient times. In the Shang dynasty (1766–1123 B.C.), the king was at the same time an archshaman, mediating the divine and the secular. Although shamanism in political contexts grew less important after the Chou dynasty (1122–256 B.C.), it has played a major role as a folk religion.[30] Since the adoption of Neo-Confucianism as the official and orthodox ideology in the Sung dynasty, all modes of overt religious behavior were considered superstition except for ancestor worship and Chan meditation. By the Ming dynasty (A.D. 1368–1644), shamanistic practices were forbidden legally as superstition. This is an attitude reinforced today in China by the combination of Western science and Marxism-Leninism.

Nonetheless, shamanism has survived by affecting and being affected by the other religions of Taoism, Confucianism, and Buddhism as the religion of the common people. According to Jordan Paper's research, in modern Hong Kong and Taiwan, a number of shamans have prospered by taking advantage of the people's wish for material success, and shamanism has thrived to the point of having a national organization.[31] Ordinary people want to protect themselves from evil spirits and to gain personal and familial well-being by means of extra-human powers. Shamanistic rituals and prayer interface with this basic human desire.

In the Korean context, shamanism has been deeply embedded in traditional Korean culture and customs throughout its long history. The particular cultural components of agrarian and fishing village festivals and ceremonies are combined with shamanistic religious rituals based on the lunar calendar. For example, the shamanistic ritual ceremony (*mudang-kut*) in Korea is essentially and traditionally a community activity. Not only does it serve to petition the gods for a better harvest or an abundant catch of fish, but also it establishes solidarity among the village people. Drinking and eating are central to the festivals for the fellowship and unity of the community.[32]

The principal function of the shaman is healing. When clients visit a shaman with their suffering and troubles, the shaman diagnoses them through spiritual communication, attributes their problems to certain evil spirits, and prescribes the use of a wide variety of charms and other symbols to exorcise the evil powers. The most effective remedy is to perform a *mudang-kut*, which is an ecstatic journey and soul flight by the shaman, accompanied by dance and music. Suh explains that the *mudang-kut* is composed of five steps: prelude, protection, exorcism, blessing, and postlude. During the ritual performance, clients go through a therapeutic process of projection, catharsis, transference, consolation, exhortation, transcendence, and redemption.[33] The main purpose is to exorcise or console the spirits that are causing the present problems.

According to Suh's research, most clients are powerless against worldly suffering and the pain caused by the political, social, and economic structure. In other words, these are the common people, the Korean *minjung*.[34] Through the process of performance, they are empowered to cope with their present suffering and problems. The *mudang-kut* has had a revitalizing power in the life of the individual and the community in Korean society and has given them an optimistic worldview by healing and promising the worldly blessings of health, wealth, and success. As such, the primary concern of shamanism is well-being in this world and human liberation from troubles caused by evil spirits.

In contemporary Korea, shamanism's traditional communal function seems to disappear as a result of industrialization and modernization. As evidence, the government makes efforts to preserve traditional folk plays and festivals as part of a disappearing cultural heritage. Shamanistic monuments and relics are in many cases treated as museum pieces. However, shamanism is still a popular faith among individual Koreans because shamanistic ideology is an expression of basic human instinct. It affirms the importance of living in this world, its main concern being the individual's wish fulfillment by the blessings of health, wealth, and success. This essence of shamanistic ideology easily corresponds to materialism and capitalism and cooperates with the basic human desire for prosperity. At this point, shamanism still exercises its influence over the religious consciousness of the people. The practice of the shaman remains popular in the individual's private life, and the *mudang-kut* is still performed as a means of blessing or prayer for one's personal or household prosperity.[35]

In Japan shamanism was also a prominent folk religion. In traditional Japan, shamans appealed to both the imperial court and the common people as the mediator communicating with the *kami*, the native Japanese deities. Throughout a long period of religious history, Japanese shamanism has commingled with Shinto and Buddhism, and its ritual practice has syncretized in many ways.[36] Particularly, Shinto rituals — based on the native religious idea that humans are dependent on the *kami*, much as children are on their parents — adopted shamanistic communication. That is, the *kami* is considered to possess the *miko*, animate her body, and speak through her mouth after making her fall into a trance.[37]

One of the distinctive characteristics of traditional Japanese shamanism, as Denise Carmody indicates, is the significant social role of the female shamans:

The *miko* were quite important to society. They tended to band together and travel a circuit of villages, primarily to act as mediums for contact with the dead but also to serve as diviners and oracles. They also ministered to spiritual and physical ills, which popular culture largely attributed to malign spirits. As a result, the *miko* developed both a poetic and a pharmacological lore. In composing songs and dances to accompany their ministrations, they contributed a great deal to the formation of traditional Japanese dance, theater, balladry, and puppetry.[38]

In contemporary Japan, shamanism exists in the common people's lives as a vital factor, and shamanistic rituals are still performed mostly in rural areas to direct the people's spiritual journey.

Likewise, shamanism, as the oldest and still effective religious phenomenon, is one of the most influential elements of the Asian worldview and ethos. Its ideology and concerns are fundamental to the religiosity of East Asians and appeal to them in various forms and styles. In the pluralistic religious context, it has commingled with such religions as Buddhism, Confucianism, and Taoism and has survived as a forceful religious element among Asians.

The Influence of Shamanism on Asian Americans

The shamanistic tradition also exerts an influence on Christianity in East Asia in several ways. First, shamanism helped Asian and Asian American Christians accept the existence of the Spirit and believe in its power in their daily lives. They perceive the Holy Spirit to be like ancestral spirits or *kami*, who are the agents through which believers can be delivered from suffering and be blessed in this world with wealth, health, and longevity. They understand that their present suffering and problems are caused by evil spirits and that the divine power of the Holy Spirit is the means of overcoming them. There is no doubt that God is working in this world through the Holy Spirit in order to liberate them from such predicaments.

In this regard, Asian American congregations want to experience the living power of the Holy Spirit in their daily lives and in preaching. Moreover, they want preaching to reflect their life issues and problems from the biblical perspective and provide them with spiritual guidelines and energy to cope with their present suffering. There-fore, Asian Christians' tendency to depend on the power of the Holy Spirit has given Asian and Asian American churches vitality and dy-namism. For them, Christian faith is realistic and concrete rather than metaphysical and abstract.

Second, this preference for spiritual experience has produced confu-sion about Christian pneumatology within Asian and Asian American churches. Many preachers tend to overemphasize spiritual experience in preaching without proper theological guidelines and thus cause spiritual confusion within the church. They understand spiritual ex-perience as the baptism of the Holy Spirit, which can be proved by speaking in tongues, miraculous healing, and answered prayer on an individual level. In order to testify about the personal experiences of the Holy Spirit, the preacher often uses the miracle stories or personal success accounts either in the Bible or in illustrations and stresses that such stories can become "our stories" by faith. As a result, preaching gives the listeners the impression that the gospel itself is a present-centered and success-oriented message. Moreover, emphasizing the power of the Holy Spirit only in relation to visible signs and miracles causes a theological crisis because such an understanding distorts the authenticity of Christian truths. In this context, one of the primary tasks of Asian American preaching is to help the congregation feel the presence of God within a proper understanding of the Christian doctrine of the Holy Spirit and to guide them in the right direction on their spiritual journey.

Last, Asian American congregations tend to see the preacher's image and authority to be like that of a shaman. They consciously or unconsciously expect their preacher to communicate with spirits and to help them cope with their problems by provoking the power of the Holy Spirit in their lives. In other words, they want the preacher to be a spiritual leader who is closer to God than they are and who can better communicate with the Holy Spirit. In this way, they often give credit to the preacher on the basis of the sermon's spiritual power to transform their whole lives. Each time they listen to the sermon, they want to be touched deeply by the Word of God so that they may confirm and renew their faith by experiencing the presence of God. This expectation by the congregation often challenges preachers to be diligent in disciplining their spirituality through prayer and biblical studies while it tends to encourage them to behave as an authoritarian leader.

External Conditions

Traditional cultural distinctiveness is not the only determining factor in the formation of the corporate ethnic personality of the Asian American congregation. Asian Americans are not isolated from the society around them. They are a part of American society; its political ideology and socioeconomic structures have affected their lives directly or indirectly. They also interact with other ethnic groups in the United States and adopt, consciously or unconsciously, various cultural elements in the process of socialization. These external relations with the larger society have contributed to producing and reproducing the particular subculture that is the Asian American congregation.

Asian immigrants who had been used to indigenous Confucian hierarchical culture in their homelands now face a fairly different cultural atmosphere grounded in the ideal of egalitarian democracy in the United States. This society challenges their mentality and lifestyle on several fronts: the enhanced social status of women and their active participation in every field of society; the dynamic interrelationships between different age groups and social ranks; and the influence of mass media and political rhetoric.

While acknowledging this positive element of American culture, the preacher must also understand the negative aspects of the external conditions of Asian American congregations. Many Asian American sermons tend to identify the prevailing ideology of egalitarian democracy with the present reality of the Asian American community, failing to distinguish between the ideal and the actual. Preachers are apt to describe the United States as God's promised land and to assume that American society is as open to Asian immigrants as it is to other Americans for achieving their life goals. Moreover, some preachers may adopt the secular concept of the American dream, which means they proclaim present, worldly blessing at a personal level in their sermons without critical theological reflection; they may stress positive thinking and faith as the means of making that dream come true. This kind of preaching can stress that if listeners are diligent and faithful to God, they will be blessed and succeed in this world physically and economically.

However, such preaching is problematic both theologically and practically. It misdirects the listeners to an individualistic self-centered faith, which is alien to biblical tradition and Reformed theology. It also prevents the congregation from realizing that their sociopolitical problems may arise from fundamental structural discrimination based on race. In this context, it is crucial for Asian American preaching to look beneath the surface of American society in order to respond faithfully to problems within the Asian American community.

The external conditions that need the preacher's special attention can be explored in relation to three aspects: historicopolitical, economic, and sociocultural problems of the Asian American community.

Prejudiced Images of Asian Americans

Although Asians were found in North America in the late eighteenth century, official immigration as a large group began in the nineteenth century. The Chinese, the first trans-Pacific immigrants, arrived in San Francisco in 1849.[39] Since then, hundreds of thousands of Chinese migrated to California in order to escape poverty and political upheaval. They were employed in such physically difficult jobs as mining, agriculture, and railroad building, and in industries such as textiles, clothing, shoes, and cigars, where they were exploited with low pay and experienced violence due to racial discrimination. They have been mistreated both legally by the anti-Chinese statutes[40] and personally by numerous hate crimes.[41]

This anti-Chinese prejudice was applied to other Asian immigrants, among them the Japanese and the Koreans. The first large group of Japanese immigrants went to Hawaii as indentured laborers and re-emigrated to the American West Coast after the annexation of Hawaii in 1898. They worked in agriculture and railroad maintenance, where they suffered from discriminatory treatment. Koreans immigrated later than did the Chinese and Japanese. When Chinese and Japanese laborers demanded better treatment in sugar and pineapple plantations in Hawaii, the government proposed importing Korean labor. In 1903, 101 contracted Korean laborers, who had been converted to Christianity by American missionaries in Korea, arrived in Honolulu. On their arrival, these immigrants established a Korean American church. Oppressive plantation life was characterized by "racial and ethnic segregation, hard work, low wages, and minimal contact with other groups," but the church played a major role in supporting the Korean immigrants spiritually as well as socially.

The common experience of harsh racial discrimination among Asian immigrants was the result of intolerance by European Americans. This majority could not accept Asians because of their visible and societal differences, from their skin color and almond eyes to values, customs, and norms of family and community. European Americans had little knowledge of the history and culture of Asians and treated them as a "problem minority."[42]

The suffering of Asian immigrants caused by racial prejudice has continued to the present day. During the World War II, Japanese Americans were discriminated against and sent to concentration camps. During the Cold War era, many Chinese Americans who had relatives in mainland China were suspected and investigated by J. Edgar Hoover's FBI and other organizations.[43] The 1965 immigration Act, which abolished the national origins system, stimulated the growth of Asian immigration.[44]

Since then some successful Asian immigrants have gained public attention. In 1982, *Newsweek* applied the catch phrase "model minority" to Asian Americans in recounting success stories of Asian immigrants.[45] Although this stereotype seems to suggest that mainstream America highly values Asian immigrants' adjustment, it also contains at least two negative implications. On the one hand, they regard Asian Americans as good models who assimilate into American life by accepting their assigned status cheerfully and not being offensive to the dominant white society.[46] On the other hand, this stereotype has led Americans to ignore that the majority of Asian immigrants are still struggling to survive in racist American society. They face such problems as an unfamiliarity with the dominant white culture, the lack of a solid socioeconomic base, and language problems.

Racial discrimination against Asian American communities is often reinforced by misinformation by the mass media. In fact, the average American is ignorant of Asian American communities beyond what they see in the print and electronic media. Unfortunately, the media have portrayed Asian Americans with bias. Out of cultural ignorance, reporters and editors of major newspapers and magazines often misinterpret Asian cultural, social, and political matters. According to a report of the U.S. Commission on Civil Rights, until the early 1970s the mainstream media depicted Asian Americans largely as citizens of Asian nations rather than as naturalized citizens. They often viewed them in a negative light only in connection with wars like World War II, the Korean War, and the Vietnam War. For example, the television series *M*A*S*H* (now seen in syndication) and the Broadway show *Miss Saigon* give Americans false images and the inadequate impression that even contemporary Korea and Vietnam are still under such inhumane social and political conditions.

Moreover, the mass media tend to describe Asian immigrants as a single stereotypical group rather than understanding their distinctive history, values, thoughts, and feelings. Popular stereotypes of Asian Americans, caricatured in American popular culture for generations, are either the "power-hungry despot, the helpless heathen, the sensuous dragon lady, the comical loyal servant, the pudgy, de-sexed detective who talks about Confucius," or "sinister villains, and brute hordes."[47] These refer to "the inferiority of people of color" and thereby perpetuate ideological justification for European American superiority.

This biased portrayal by the media has encouraged anti-Asian prejudice and discrimination, resulting in numerous hate crimes against Asian immigrant communities. For example, the Los Angeles riots of 1992 revealed that Koreans were blamed or scapegoated for the economic frustrations of African Americans. Numerous other hate crimes against the Korean immigrant community have been committed, reported or unreported. According to Andrew Sung Park,

in August 1993 a man shot a Korean-American grocer in Washington, D.C., took a potato chip package, and walked out slowly. It was surmised that the motive was not robbery but racial hatred. In the same month someone broke into a Korean-American house at Rowland

Heights, California, and left a burned swastika and racially insulting graffiti on a rug and a wall inside. About the same time, a New York policeman hurled racial epithets at a young Korean-American woman and then hit her. Her "crime" was a parking violation. . . . [48]

This racist context for Asian Americans challenges the preacher to reflect on working toward a reconciliation with other ethnic groups in the United States. The distorted image of Asian American communities, fostered by personal and communal misunderstandings, and the misinformed and prejudiced reports of media and other public communications can be corrected. The restoration of undistorted images of Asian American communities requires of preachers dual theological tasks. On the one hand, the preacher critiques the white-dominant culture of America by discerning and deconstructing the dehumanizing myths that have prevailed in popular American society. On the other hand, the preacher reconstructs positive images of Asian Americans on the basis of knowledge and information about the community. Telling the authentic stories of Asian history, culture, and Christian identity in preaching will provide the listeners not only with a positive self-affirmation but also with a communal vision for American society.

This kind of preaching, heard by other ethnic congregations as well as by Asian American listeners, will shatter those discriminatory stereotypes prevailing in popular American society. In this regard, second- and third-generation Asian American preachers whose native language is English are challenged to build a bridge between Asian and other ethnic groups in the United States through preaching the vision of the Christian church in God's future promise.

Economic Globalization and Unequal Distribution of Wealth

The American economic system is fundamentally based on capitalism. The current tendency is toward monopoly capitalism and what American managers call the logic of the global marketplace. Mergers have enabled many large corporations to preserve profits, thereby becoming even larger and establishing monopoly capitalism. As they survey this worldwide arena, these companies are encouraged to relocate their industrial production to countries with lower labor costs.

As a result, millions of skilled blue-collar employees in North America have lost jobs, leaving only one-fifth of all Americans — those in such international demand as lawyers, biotechnology engineers, economists, software designers, strategic planners, and stockbrokers — to enjoy the benefits of globalization.[49]

This economic condition has widened the gap between rich and poor. Doug Henwood criticizes North America for having "the smallest middle class and the highest poverty rates in the First world."[50] According to one statistic, on average managers earn more than ninety times as much as do industrial workers. The Internal Revenue Service in 1989 reported that 1 percent of the population controlled 37 percent of the nation's wealth (up from 31 percent in 1983) and that 10 percent of the population controlled 86 percent of the wealth. In 1993, 15.1 percent were below the official government poverty level. According to a 1994 report, 10 percent of the total population were hungry or depended on soup kitchens or food stamps.[51] Thirty percent of African Americans and 20 percent of Hispanics fall below the official poverty line and live in slums.[52]

At the same time that the unequal distribution of wealth widens the gap between rich and poor and fosters economic recession, political campaigns have also exploited poor immigrants, blaming them for economic recession and slow economic growth. Propaganda tends to point to the immigrants as welfare beneficiaries and fosters in the minds of the majority a negative image of new immigrants. Moreover, many Americans often insist that Asian and other immigrants steal jobs from them.[53]

In this economic and political situation, most Asian immigrants are marginalized and victimized. Although they struggle hard, the average Asian immigrant falls into the lower or lower middle class in income.[54] They work hard just to stay even, which leads to increased stress and sometimes workplace injuries. New immigrants are relegated to living as second-class citizens. They are shut out of the mainstream because of a language barrier, a lack of job information, and the racist and exclusionary nature of the industries that supply better jobs. New immigrants accept jobs at a very low wage for service employment or survive in sweatshops, regardless of their education and occupational experience in their home countries.[55]

Old immigrants also have a hard time surviving in a competitive economic condition. According to one statistic, more than 50 percent of the adult Korean immigrants operate self-employed retail or small businesses.[56] They often compete with other minorities, and when the competition becomes fierce, racial tensions flare. It is also hard for those who have professional jobs to survive in racist economic conditions. They either become surplus labor or soon run into the glass ceiling in employment, leaving them discouraged, left out of society, and feeling like failures.[57]

In this context, Asian American congregations need to realize that individual success cannot be gained unless this American economic system and its values are transformed for the common well-being. As long as an unequal system and unjust structures prevail in the American economy, there is little or no hope for economic prosperity within new immigrant communities. Such structural problems of the American economic system challenge Asian American preachers to ponder the concept of "economic democracy,"[58] to consider a different set of values for establishing the kind of society we would have, and to fight against the abuses of the system from the perspective of the Christian gospel.

This vision for the kingdom of God relativizes our present economic system in which the gap between rich and poor is great and challenges Christians to develop a new model in which those who have been hired late "for his vineyard" will earn "the usual daily wage" equal to that of all others (Matthew 20:1–16). Asian American preaching grounded in this eschatological vision will transform the secular concept of the American dream and stimulate the listeners to cooperate in making Christ's vision come true within and beyond the Asian American community.

Cultural Imperialism and Identity Crisis

American society is dominated by Eurocentric culture. The home-country values and morals of immigrants clash with those of America. Differences in habits, customs, and language make immigrants feel psychologically restricted and emotionally imprisoned in the American social context. They often lose or confuse values and the meaning of life. For non-European immigrants, the prerequisite for becoming American has been to leave one's culture at the door. Whether young or old, educated or ignorant, rich or poor, all have to go through resocialization, a process of value change, role redefinition, and the learning of new and modified behaviors under a new self-image.

Asian immigrants are no exception. This resocialization process has required them to expend enormous energy; perseverance in the process has led Asian immigrants to feel conflict, anxiety, dissatisfaction, and frustration. This is aggravated by two problems. First, American public services cannot help new immigrants sufficiently to settle into their new land. Many Asian immigrants arrive in the United States with little background information about American society. They need professional bilingual and bicultural counseling services to help them in their personal, social, and academic development. Such services, however, do not exist for most Asian immigrants. Asian immigrant children in the public schools are unable to use counseling services because of the limited availability of bilingual, bicultural counselors.[59] A lack of services for new immigrants' children in the public schools increases the chance of dropping out among Asian immigrant high school students. According to statistics, the dropout rates for students who speak a language other than English are twice as high as they are for those whose primary language is English. Moreover, Asian Americans are discouraged from using the courts by a lack of court interpreters. Bilingual court interpreters are not always available to facilitate understanding for those who are not fluent in English. Asian Americans make up only 0.7 percent of the lawyers nationwide, although they constitute 2.9 percent of the population.[60]

Second, Eurocentric American culture has fostered European American superiority in the minds of the majority so that they do not respect other ethnic cultures. Public school education focuses on a European American way of life, giving great weight to European history, culture, religion, and language, and does not provide sufficient knowledge or appreciation of Asian values, history, or culture. This kind of school education not only fosters ignorance by American people about Asia and undermines of Asian immigrant self-esteem, but also it contributes to conflicts between immigrant parents and children. Children who are exposed to the Western-based value systems stressing individuality and autonomy are often in conflict with the Asian ways of family and community centeredness, interdependence, and harmony taught at home.

Furthermore, cultural imperialism in American society results in an identity crisis among Asian immigrants. The question of Who am I? is intensely problematic at a certain stage of an immigrant's life. The lack of life satisfaction (psychological) and job satisfaction (socioeconomic achievement) increases this identity crisis. When immigrants feel that the dominant group will never fully accept them and that the United States is a racist society for them, they experience marginality, and their marginal situation creates anxiety, confusion, and insecurity.[61] Faced with this identity crisis, first-generation Asian immigrants have a double identity. They regard themselves as temporary sojourners in American society, considering the possibility of going back to their homelands in the near future. This double status leads them to exclude themselves from American society and discourages them from any interaction with other ethnic groups. This tendency not only deprives them of an opportunity to extend themselves into mainstream America but also weakens their responsibility as Asian American citizens. They simply see themselves as a sacrificial generation for their children. Although they may never become full citizens, they endure suffering caused by racism in the hope that their children will have an identity as American citizens, with full access to economic, political, and social opportunities.

However, Asian American children growing up in America cannot meet their parents' and grandparents' expectations to embody this American identity because fundamental, structural discrimination and racial prejudice are too great to transcend. Although they were born in the United States and have already accepted the dominant American culture as a norm for their lives, they experience an identity crisis more profound than that of the first generation. They feel themselves neither Asian nor American.[62] While they identify themselves with Americans, they cannot be fully integrated into European American culture because of their outward appearance and inward cultural ethos. No matter how well they might be assimilated into American culture, they are often treated as Asians or foreigners by other Americans. They are psychologically vulnerable to the unspoken question Why don't you go back to where you came from?[63] This popular racist attitude among majority Americans frustrates Asian Americans. In this predicament, Asian American children constantly struggle to give meaning and labels to their self-identity.

This reality awakens Asian American preaching to the urgent need for a contextualized theology for Asian immigrant communities that can provide theological guidelines for dealing with racist cultural problems, including the identity crisis. When Asian American preaching is grounded in such a theological perspective, it will help the listeners build a self-affirming and positive identity within the community of faith. Furthermore, when its concerns are extended to a reform of the structural problems of American culture, it can influence American politicians and educators. Through its message, they may realize the significance of society's pluralistic and multicultural trends and learn about immigrant students' cultural backgrounds and needs. A more culturally balanced educational curricula can hold the interest of all students; teaching Asian history, language, religion, and culture in public schools will provide all Americans with knowledge about Asian Americans and at the same time help Asian Americans understand and take pride in their roots. This should be a focus in churches, and such an effort would promote inclusiveness in American culture and enhance cross-cultural relationships in American society.

Conclusion

The preceding examination of the internal and external conditions of Asian American congregations reveals that they have been greatly influenced by their native religious and cultural traditions. The traditional religions of shamanism, Buddhism, and Confucianism have contributed to the formation of the corporate personality of the Asian American community. Their influence is present in all aspects of Christian life, including preaching and worship. The preacher cannot ignore these traditional aspects of the congregation because they not only provide the context for preaching but also function as rich resources for the development of Asian American preaching. The preacher's task is to discern the traditional religious forces within the congregation and to use them critically and effectively for the sake of proclaiming the Christian gospel.

Our discussion of internal and external conditions also reveals that Asian American congregations are under enormous stress psychologically, physically, and emotionally because of racial prejudice and a perverse social system. They have been struggling to survive in Eurocentric American culture, yearning for the transformation of society into an inclusive environment. In this scenario, society would no longer dominated by the ideologies of Eurocentricity, but all Americans, minority and majority alike, would live cooperatively. In this congregational context, Asian American preaching is responsible for building an inclusive society within and beyond the ethnic community. It is challenged to provide an authentic vision for the community of faith from a Christian theological perspective. This vision encourages listeners to work to transform the community through positive interaction and corporate relationships with other ethnic groups.

Based on this background, the following four chapters will concentrate on the development of a set of homiletical strategies for Asian American preaching. They will address these homiletical categories: the theology of preaching, biblical interpretation, the sermonic form, and the language of preaching.

Notes

1. Thomas G. Long, *The Witness of Preaching* (Louisville: Westminster/ John Knox, 1989), 22–23.
2. James F. Hopewell, *Congregation: Stories and Structures* (Philadelphia: Fortress, 1987), 15.
3. Long, 131.
4. C. Ellis Nelson, *Congregations: Their Power to Form and Transform* (Atlanta: John Knox, 1988), 7.
5. Kenneth Uyeda Fong, *Insights for Growing Asian-American Ministries* (Rosemead, Calif.: Evergrowing Publications, 1990), 68.
6. See Jung Young Lee, *Korean Preaching: An Interpretation* (Nashville: Abingdon, 1997). Taoism is also one of representative religions of East Asia. Its distinctive elements have influenced and been mixed with three other indigenous religions in their theories and practices.

7. Peter Nosco, "Confucian Thought: Neo-Confucianism," in *The Encyclopedia of Religion*, ed. Mircea Eliade (New York: Macmillan, 1987), 4:17.

8. Julia Ching, *Chinese Religions* (Maryknoll, N.Y.: Orbis, 1993), 84–89; Dong-Shik Ryu, *The Christian Faith Encounters the Religions of Korea* (Seoul: The Christian Literature Society of Korea, 1965), 68.

9. Nosco, 4:35.

10. JaHyun K. Haboush, "The Confucianization of Korean Society," in *The East Asian Region: Confucian Heritage and Its Modern Adaptation*, ed. G. Rozman (Princeton, N.J.: Princeton University Press, 1991), 93, 109–10.

11. JaHyun K. Haboush, "Confucianism in Korea," in *The Encyclopedia of Religion*, ed. Mircea Eliade, 4:14.

12. The information in this paragraph is from Peter Nosco, "Confucianism in Japan," in *The Encyclopedia of Religion*, ed. Mircea Eliade, 4:7–9, 10.

13. Won Moo Hurh and Kwang Chung Kim, *Korean Immigrants in America: Structural Analysis of Ethnic Confinement and Adhesive Adaptation* (Rutherford, N.J.: Fairleigh Dickinson University Press, 1984), 55, 58. According to this book, Korean Americans are the most highly educated group in the United States and "hard workers." In 1970, 71 percent of Korean Americans completed high school and 36 percent completed college, whereas only 11 percent of the total population were college graduates. In 1978 only 1.3 percent of Koreans were divorced or separated.

14. Fong, 46.

15. Ibid., 130.

16. Minza Kim Boo, "The Social Reality of the Korean-American Women: Toward Crashing with the Confucian Ideology," in *Korean-American Women: Toward Self-Realization*, ed. Inn Sook Lee (Mansfield, Ohio: The Association of Korean Christian Scholars in North America, 1985), 68.

17. Inn Sook Lee, "Women's Emancipation Movement Within the Christian Context," in *Korean-American Women: Toward Self-Realization*, ed. Inn Sook Lee (Mansfield, Ohio: The Association of Korean Christian Scholars in North America, 1985), 111.

18. Ibid., 84.

19. Boo, 93.

20. Denise L. Carmody and John T. Carmody, *Eastern Ways to the Center: An Introduction to the Religions of Asia* (Belmont, Calif.: Wadsworth, 1992), 68. The Eightfold Path can be summarized as follows. Right views are the knowledge of the Four Noble Truths. Right intention is dispassion, benevolence, and refusal to injure others. Right speech means not lying, slandering, abusing, and talking in idleness. Right action means not taking life, stealing, and being sexually disordered. Right livelihood means having an occupation that does not harm living thing. Thus, butchers, hunters, fishers, and sellers

of weapons or liquor are proscribed. Right effort is to avoid evil thoughts. Right mindfulness is to discipline oneself to focus on the essential reality of an object or idea. Right concentration is to concentrate on a worthy object of meditation.

21. Frank Reynolds and Charles Hallisey, "Buddhism: An Overview," in *The Encyclopedia of Religion*, ed. Mircea Eliade, 2:341.

22. Robert G. Orr, *Religion in China* (New York: Friendship Press, 1980), 109.

23. Reynolds and Hallisey, 341; Ryu, 43–44.

24. David Kwang-sun Suh, "Minjung Theology: The Politics and Spirituality of Korean Christianity," in *Perspectives on Christianity in Korea and Japan: The Gospel and Culture in East Asia*, ed. Mark R. Mullins and Richard Fox Young (Lewiston, N.Y.: Edwin Mellen Press, 1995), 150–51.

25. Robert E. Buswell Jr., "Buddhism in Korea," in *The Encyclopedia of Religion*, ed. Mircea Eliade, 2:422.

26. Suh, 153.

27. Tamaru Noriyoshi, "Buddhism in Japan," in *The Encyclopedia of Religion*, ed. Mircea Eliade, 2:426.

28. Ibid., 432.

29. Suh, 91.

30. Mu-chou Poo, *In Search of Personal Welfare: A View of Ancient Chinese Religion* (New York: State University of New York Press, 1998), 24, 52.

31. Jordan Paper, *The Spirits Are Drunk* (New York: State University of New York Press, 1998), 120.

32. Suh, 96.

33. Ibid., 108–9.

34. Ibid., viii, 23, 110. The word *minjung* is a combination of two Chinese characters, *min*, which means "people," and *jung*, which means "the mass." They are understood to be the people who have been oppressed economically, socially, politically, or sexually in the long history of Korea.

35. Ibid., 121–23.

36. B. Byron Earhart, *Religion in the Japanese Experience: Sources and Interpretations* (Encino, Calif.: Dickenson, 1974), 95–96.

37. Robert K. C. Forman, ed., *Religions of Asia* (New York: St. Martin's Press, 1993), 203.

38. Carmody and Carmody, 148.

39. Harry H. L. Kitano and Roger Daniels, *Asian-Americans: Emerging Minorities* (Englewood Cliffs, N.J.: Prentice-Hall, 1988), 19.

40. Ibid., 22–23. The California Constitution of 1879 barred the Chinese from employment and ownership of land. The Chinese Exclusion Act of 1882 barred the immigration of Chinese laborers for ten years, and the act was made permanent in 1902.

41. James C. Thomson Jr., Peter W. Stanley, and John Curtis Perry, *Sentimental Imperialists: The American Experience in East Asia* (San Francisco: Harper & Row, 1981), 85–92. Many early Chinese Americans were without legal protection, shot or lynched, even battered to death or burned alive by European Americans.

42. The information in this and the preceding paragraph is from Kitano and Daniels, 71, 108 (the quoted matter).

43. Ibid., 42.

44. For example, Korean immigration into the United States has skyrocketed since that year, and nearly a million Koreans were residing in the United States by 1990. More than 80 percent of them arrived after 1965. See Jung Ha Kim, *Bridge-Makers and Cross-Bearers: Korean-American Women and the Church* (Atlanta: Scholars Press, 1997), 7.

45. *Newsweek*, December 6, 1982, quoted from Kitano and Daniels, 48. It is said that sociologist William Peterson first applied this phrase only to Japanese Americans in 1966.

46. Elaine H. Kim, *Asian-American Literature: An Introduction to the Writings and Their Social Context* (Philadelphia: Temple University Press, 1982), 18–19.

47. Ibid., 3.

48. Andrew Sung Park, *Racial Conflict and Healing: An Asian-American Theological Perspective* (Maryknoll, N.Y.: Orbis, 1996), 28.

49. Paul Kennedy, *Preparing for the Twenty-first Century* (New York: Vintage, 1993), 59.

50. Doug Henwood, "American Dream: It's Not Working," *Christianity and Crisis* 52 (1992): 195.

51. Quoted from Park, 38; Cornel West, *Race Matters* (New York: Vintage, 1994), 10–11.

52. Kennedy, 304.

53. *Civil Rights: Civil Rights Issues Facing Asian Americans in the 1990s, a Report of the United States Commission on Civil Rights* (Washington, D.C., February 1992), 182.

54. For example, according to the statistics, the average Korean household income in Los Angeles was $16,610, while the overall average was $17,751. Asian Pacific Research and Development Council, "Asian Pacific Sketchbook," Los Angeles *Herald Examiner*, May 6–27, 1988, quoted from Fong, 43.

55. Park, 23–24.

56. Hurh and Kim, 115.

57. *Civil Rights*, 19.

58. William Tabb, "The Crisis of the Present Economic System and

Renewing the American Dream," in *Theology in the Americas: Detroit II Conference Papers*, ed. Cornel West, Caridad Guidote, and Margaret Coakley (Maryknoll, N.Y.: Orbis, 1982), 31.

59. Harry H. L. Kitano, "A Model for Counseling Asian Americans," in *Counseling Across Cultures*, ed. Paul B. Pederson et al. (Honolulu: University of Hawaii Press, 1989), 140.

60. *Civil Rights*, 72 (for statistics about dropout rates), 173.

61. Hurh and Kim, 140.

62. See Joann Faung Jean Lee, ed., *Asian Americans* (New York: The New Press, 1991).

63. Elaine H. Kim, 72.

Chapter Two

A Theology of Preaching

The internal and external conditions of Asian American congregations, which were explored in the previous chapter, reveal that one of the major tasks of Asian American homiletics is to develop a new theological perspective for preaching from the particular experience of Asian American congregations. They, as an ethnic minority in the United States, experience a "loss of home" in the pluralistic society and uncertainty about their future living with the racism found in this country. Having set forth into a new land by either choice or necessity, they are strangers in the land. At the same time, they are pioneers, strengthened by the biblical faith that they are not alone but are surrounded by a cloud of witnesses.[1] This experience challenges the preacher to concentrate on the following theological questions: What is preaching? Why is it necessary for the Asian American community? What is the image of the preacher and his or her role in the community of faith?

Asian American congregations are waiting for contextually relevant theological responses to these questions. They expect that sermons they hear every Sunday to reflect critically on their particular life experience and to provide them with a theological direction for their spiritual lives. In this regard, it is crucial to discuss those theological issues of preaching in relation to Christian spirituality. An understanding of the nature and function of preaching and the image and role of the preacher cannot be separated from the formation and nurture of the spirituality of Asian American congregations.

Both inside and beyond the church the term *spirituality* is much in vogue. Its ambiguity remains problematic. The term is one of the most confusing and complicated words that has been employed to describe everything from Christian meditation, New Age practices, and pop psychology to various forms of Asian mysticism such as yoga,

Zen meditation, prayer groups, and retreats in the desert. These understandings of spirituality are based on private experiences and are not very helpful in developing a theology of preaching. By contrast, referring to 1 Corinthians 2, the word *spirituality* linguistically suggests a lifestyle "under the leadership of the Holy Spirit"[2] or a living relationship with the Holy Spirit. Still, the implications of this word are many because the meaning of spiritual life is understood variously within different historical and theological contexts. The definition of spirituality is contextual. It is not a fixed doctrinal concept but is open to the changing situation of human life.

In this regard, Asian American homiletics is challenged to develop a meaning of Christian spirituality by relating the particular experience of its congregation to a certain theological perspective. The method of searching for the spirituality of the Asian American congregation is dialogically dialectical. First, it attempts to describe the distinctive spiritual elements composing Asian American ethnic spirituality. Asian Americans' lifestyle and goals are lived according to a certain conviction about the nature and purpose of human life. They are formed with the influence of spiritual and transcendental experiences based on traditional religious and cultural interaction between the individual and his or her community. Second, the characteristics of Asian American ethnic spirituality relate to dialogue with Christian tradition and theology and therefore possess some corresponding elements in Christian apocalyptic eschatology. From this dialogue between Asian spirituality and Christian eschatology a distinctive Christian spirituality emerges.

The theology of Asian American preaching is concerned with Christian spirituality and understands preaching to be spiritual preaching. An eschatological perspective redefines the nature and function of preaching and the image and role of the preacher. However, it is important to keep in mind that just as the concept of spirituality is not established in a final form so long as there is life and the possibility of new experience and new learning, the theology of preaching that is related to Christian spirituality is not static but is in a dynamic process of development.

For the purpose of arriving at a theology of preaching, this chapter includes three parts: first, the investigation of the characteristics of Asian American ethnic spirituality; second, an understanding of Christian spirituality based on the theological implications of Asian spirituality; and last, the development of spiritual preaching as the theology of preaching. From an understanding of this distinctive Christian spirituality, the nature and function of preaching and the image and role of the preacher will be discussed.

Asian Spirituality

In Asian terminology, the corresponding word for spirituality may be *tao*, which means the way of human life. It includes a certain understanding of the goal of life and a lifestyle in pursuit of that goal. It includes such internal and external elements of human lives as religious practices, traditional customs, worldview, values of life, morality, and so forth. In this sense, it is not an overstatement to say that indigenous religions and popular culture have contributed a great deal to the development of Asian spirituality. The syncretistic and co-existing elements of Confucianism, Buddhism, and shamanism over thousands of years in East Asia have influenced popular culture and nurtured a particular Asian lifestyle. Asian spirituality is so broad and multifaceted that it is hard to limit its description to several points. Nevertheless, the following section attempts to introduce Asian spirituality in a general way by exploring three key aspects — critical transcendence, spiritual sensibility, and the sense of communality. It aims to generate a productive theological discussion in order to develop an understanding of Asian American Christian spirituality.

Critical Transcendence

The co-existence of Confucian humanity, Buddhist soteriology, and shamanistic wish-fulfillment in the Asian religious context have provided Asian spirituality with an optimistic worldview. That is, although Asians accept the notion that life involves suffering, they understand suffering not to be the final word. They believe that suffering will turn into a blessing because human existence is fundamentally good and holds a wonderful potential.

As a way to overcome suffering, Buddhism teaches us to deny material cravings and to become wholly spiritual. How, then, have Asians overcome suffering when it was caused by unjust political and economic systems? Asian history and culture reveal that oppressed people did not suffer passively but actively resisted the injustice of rulers and social systems. Their resistance grew out of the firm conviction that evil power would perish soon because it was against the will of heaven.

Young-Hak Hyun, a pioneer of minjung theology, discovers the spiritual power of resistance among oppressed people, minjung, in their popular culture. When the minjung felt a sense of helplessness, a feeling of abandonment (*han*), they neither easily fell into despair nor gave up on their lives. Instead, they developed a capacity for transcending their present suffering by developing such various cultural performances as the puppet show, *pansori* (one-person opera), and mask dance. Hyun finds a distinctive Asian spirituality especially in the performance of the mask dance drama in which the main character, a clown, provokes laughter and tears.

> In the mask dance the minjung make fun of people. First, they ridicule an old Buddhist monk who represents Buddhism, the so-called higher religion, senile and idealistic, impotent to procreate or provide anything concrete for the life of the peasants. Secondly, they play jokes on the ruling aristocratic literati who pretend to be learned and respectable but do not understand what is happening in reality and therefore incompetent and yet beat up the minjung. Lastly, they enact the rottenness of their own lot in this world with tears and laughter. A couple who were separated in their youth, after years of hardship looking for each other, finally come together. But finding that the old man has a young concubine the old woman gets into a fight and gets killed. A shaman performs a funeral ritual so that her soul may go to heaven.... In all this you can hear the minjung saying, "What da h— is this? After getting the worst deal in this g— d— world, still what you get in death is only a shaman's prayer?" You can see the tears on their faces and hear their laughter at the same time.... They experience transcendence not only over the world controlled by their enemies but over the total history including their own religion. They seem even to put their own lot and the religion "under the judgment of God."[3]

As Hyun interprets this drama, the minjung are the audience of the drama but at the same time have no distance from the characters in the play. Rather, they identify themselves with the characters and participate in the performance by responding actively with shouting, exclaiming, laughing, and crying. Watching that performance is cathartic for the minjung. They gain a spiritual power to cope with their present suffering and to continue their lives with hope in this unjust world. Hyun calls this spirituality "a critical transcendence."[4] It is "a liberating spirituality, a powerful political exorcism acting upon the evil spirits of oppression, exploitation, and alienation," as David K. Suh explains.[5] This transcendental experience was also the source of the revolutionary power of the minjung. Korean history reveals that whenever Korea was invaded by Japan, Mongolia, and China, the minjung organized such guerilla forces as *Manjuk-Dang, Hwalbin-Dang,* and *Donghak-Dang* and resisted them.[6] The powerless people struggled to bring justice and hope into the world by transcending their present suffering and hardship with a vision for the future.

This critical transcendence in Asian spirituality is also seen in a Chinese folktale, *The Tears of Lady Meng:*

> This happened in the reign of the wicked, unjust Emperor Ch'in Shih Huang-ti. He was afraid at this time that the Huns would break into the country from the north and not leave him any peace. In order to keep them in check, he decided to build a wall along the whole northern frontier of China. But no sooner was one piece built than another fell down, and the wall made no progress. Then a wise (!) man said to him: "A wall like this, which is over ten thousand miles long, can be built only if you immure a human being in every mile of the wall. Each mile will then have its guardian." It was easy for the Emperor to follow this advice, for he regarded his subjects as so much grass and weeds, and the whole land began to tremble under this threat. Plans were then made for human sacrifice in great numbers, at the last minute "an ingenious scholar" suggested to the Emperor that it would be sufficient to sacrifice a man called Wan "since Wan means ten thousand." Soldiers were dispatched at once to seize Wan who was sitting with his bride at the wedding feast. He was carried off by the heartless soldiers, leaving Lady Meng, his bride, in tears. Eventually, heedless of the fatigues of the journey, she traveled over mountains and through rivers to find the bones of her husband. When she saw the stupendous wall she did not know how to find the bones. There was nothing to be done, and she sat down and wept. Her weeping so affected the wall that it collapsed and laid bare her husband's bones. When the Emperor heard of Meng Chiang and how she was seeking her husband, he wanted to see her himself. When she was brought before him, her unearthly

beauty so struck him that he decided to make her Empress. She knew she could not avoid her fate, and therefore she agreed on three conditions. First, a festival lasting forty-nine days should be held in honor of her husband; second, the Emperor, with all his officials, should be present at the burial; and third, he should build a terrace forty-nine feet high on the bank of river, where she wanted to make a sacrifice to her husband.... Ch'in Shih Huang-ti granted all her requests at once. When everything was ready she climbed on to the terrace and began to curse the Emperor in a loud voice for all his cruelty and wickedness. Although this made the Emperor very angry, he held his peace. But when she jumped from the terrace into the river, he flew into a rage and ordered his soldiers to cut up her body into little pieces and grind her bones to powder. When they did this, the little pieces changed into little silverfish, in which the soul of faithful Meng Chiang lives forever.[7]

C. S. Song finds in this story the authentic Asian spirituality. He understands that the strength of the powerless derives from their bone-chilling experience of injustice and that their tears, which flow from a heart and soul that long for justice and love, generate spiritual power with which they can resist evil powers. Lady Meng's curse to the emperor in public was an indictment of the exploiting evil power against the weak. Her challenge to the power of death uncovered the disguised truth of the evil powers in the world. Yet, her death was not the end of the story. The pieces of her dead body turned into little living fish, symbolizing the power of eternal life. Her spiritual power became a seed of liberation of the oppressed.[8]

As we see in the Korean mask dance drama and the Chinese folktale, Asian spirituality is based on the critical transcendence that orients one toward an eschatological vision for the future in which all unjust suffering and hardship will cease. Asians have overcome their present oppression by critically transcending it with the spirit of resistance.

This spirituality has been passed down to Asians over the generations through the popular culture of folktales, folk songs, folk drama, and folk dance, and it also exists in Asian American spirituality as a sustaining spiritual power. Although their present life is painful as a minority immigrant group in Eurocentric American society, they transcend and resist their suffering and hardship with a vision of a better society in the future. This spirituality provides their daily lives with transcendent vitality.

Spiritual Sensibility

The syncretization of indigenous religions provides Asians with a dualistic anthropological view. For Asians, humans are a synthesis of the flesh and spirit, the finite and the infinite, and the temporal and the eternal. This view originated from a combination of the Buddhist concept of heaven and hell and of the shamanistic view of the spirits. It is believed that after death one becomes a ghost or a spirit and goes either to heaven, where the *bodhisattvas* live, or hell, which is full of tortures. Until they reach either place, the spirits wander in the human world and need to be cared for by humans. The spirits are unfathomable and mysterious. They bring harm when they are not cared for by their living relatives.[9] Confucianism adopted this understanding of the spirits and practiced ancestor worship as a way to care for the spirits of the dead for the sake of the offspring's well-being.

This anthropological view has led Asians to acknowledge the existence of spirits in the human world and their supernatural power operating their lives. Many Asians believe that human life is propelled by a principle beyond human power and knowledge and that it is supposed to promote harmony between the divine and the human. This spiritual sensibility also exists in the mentality of many Asian Americans. They have intimate feelings of spirits in their daily lives and tend to understand the power of spirits as real. Whereas this Asian view of spirits has helped Asian American Christians understand the existence of God as a form of the Spirit, it has also caused them to confuse the nature and function of the Holy Spirit with those of spirits. At this point, the Asian American homiletic needs to clarify the theological concept of the Holy Spirit in order to develop a theologically precise, relevant understanding of Christian spirituality.

The Sense of Communality

Traditional religious teachings have greatly influenced Asian American spirituality. The common fundamental goal of these teachings is to pursue harmony and unity within the universe. The universe is seen as an organic whole, with the human being as one integral part. The most typical example of this is the yin-yang theory, which emphasizes bipolar aspects of the universal principle. By inserting oneself into the interrelatedness of the universe, the individual participates in achieving universal harmony, rhythm, and balance.[10]

Muneo J. Yoshikawa distinguishes this universal and holistic essence of the Asian worldview from that of West. He explains that the Western view regards the world as "the sum of its parts" and the individual as "a separate being," while the Asian view sees the world as an "organic unity in which all things are interrelated to one another" and the individual as "a relational being." In this Asian worldview, the universe is conceived of as "a system of inseparable, interacting and ever-moving components with the individual being an integral part of this system."[11] This holistic view is the foundation of Asian spirituality. Its primary concern is communal and relational, extending from the individual to the community and to all of nature. This community-centered spirituality is represented in Confucian and Buddhist teachings and in shamanistic rituals.

In Confucianism, particularly Neo-Confucianism, spirituality can be discussed in relation to the concept of humanity. It is part of *tao*, the way of life.[12] Its essence is in interconnectedness. It emphasizes oneness and universal harmony through interdependence and reciprocity. With respect to communal human relationships, humanity means "warm human fellow feeling" or "love" in the sense of altruism or Christian love. Although the foundation of this humanity is something believed to be possessed naturally and originally from birth, it has the potential for continuous self-cultivation through human relationships.[13] As we saw in chapter 1, Confucius emphasized the primary five human relationships as a way of self-cultivation. These are means of overcoming one's self-centeredness and achieving humanity.[14] The idea of Confucian humanity as a road to universal harmony and balance within the community remains implicit in Asian spirituality and is reflected in every aspect of Asian life.

Buddhist teaching is also universal and holistic. Although Zen Buddhism tends to be understood as a private, mystic religion emphasizing an introspective and meditative state of mind, the goal of

Buddhism goes beyond that. That is, enlightenment, which means entering *nirvana*, is a condition of being achieved by eliminating the individual's self-centeredness. Enlightenment is fully realized only when it is transformed into compassionate deeds to the community. Through meditation and devotions, individual practitioners overcome the separation of being from the universe and gain oneness, or universal harmony.[15] It is exemplified in Pure Land Buddhism, which is a religion of the masses, by the life of the *bodhisattvas* who chose to live and work in the dark reality of this world for the benefit of others, refusing to reside in a transcendent, light-filled realm.[16] The Buddhist idea of communal well-being is reinforced through the process of syncretization with Confucianism and shamanism. Particularly in the Korean context, as June-Ock Yum points out, Buddhism was "transformed into something less metaphysical but more . . . capable of bringing about welfare and happiness" to believers and their relatives.[17] As a result, private meditation was extended to include a prayer for the well-being of family, society, and nature.

The communal sense of spirituality is found in shamanism, too. Contemporary shamanist ideology tends to reduce the goal of spirituality to the individual's worldly blessings, and this goal is achieved by controlling or influencing the spirits of the deceased. However, historic, traditional shamanism's more profound purpose was to achieve communal well-being and universal harmony.[18] This was well demonstrated in the shaman's role. The major role of the shaman is to heal broken relationships among human beings, between human beings and the spirits, and between humans and nature. The purpose of shamanistic rituals is to restore those broken relationships. In traditional shamanism, that ritual was essentially a community activity in which villagers gathered and pleaded for universal harmony with nature and their neighbors. It contributed to the establishment of communal solidarity.[19]

This communal sense, grounded in a holistic cosmological view, is the essence of Asian American ethnic spirituality. The pursuit of harmonious unity by solidarity and interdependent relationships with others and with nature is significant in the contemporary Asian American context. Many Asian Americans experience broken relationships caused by their shift to a radically individualistic value system and the presence of racial prejudice in society, and this sense of communality can become part of an Asian American Christian spirituality.

Theological Implications for Developing Christian Spirituality

Spirituality has been understood in various ways in the Christian tradition. They can be summarized in mystical, moral, and charismatic terms. First, the mystical view can be traced in the monastic movements of the East in the early church period. The first Christian monks and nuns from the fourth to the sixth century made a pilgrimage to the deserts and wilderness regions of Egypt, Palestine, and Syria in order to gain an ascetic and mystical experience of God.[20]

The ascetic and mystical lifestyle, an abandonment of public life in its quest for holiness, is also seen among medieval nuns and monks. They renounced the world's sensory experiences and sought an inward experience of the Spirit through the self-discipline of meditation and contemplation in monasteries. For them, Christian spirituality meant journeying into the interior mysteries of the individual soul as a way of arriving at God.[21] This mystical view is based on the Platonic dualism of soul and body. Its primary interest is in a practitioner's subjective spiritual experience apart from the secular, social, and communal experience of the self. This type of spirituality is still prominent in the Roman Catholic Church.[22]

Second, the moral view of spirituality is associated with pietist movements in the church. Since the fourteenth century, a pietist movement spread into Europe. It rejected a mystical and speculative understanding of spiritual life and emphasized both "the practical service of God and neighbor" and "humility and other holy affections" in daily lives.[23] During and after the Reformation, spirituality was no longer a term applied only to the lifestyle of monks and nuns, but it extended to the spiritual life of the laity. Martin Luther's doctrine of the priesthood of believers and John Calvin's doctrine of sanctification helped to bring Christian spirituality into the context of everyday Christian lives.[24] The saint was now understood to be an ordinary believer sanctified by God and living and praying in the world in preparation for a perfect heavenly life.

In Protestant pietism and Puritanism, an intimate fellowship with Christ was emphasized as the core of spirituality, and it was exercised at both an individual and a group level through meditation, prayer, and Scripture reading in daily rounds. A dualistic worldview, well described in American Puritan spirituality by an "exodus image" of wilderness life or a "pilgrimage of soul" in this world, stressed moral perfection as a means of daily preparation for the otherworldly life.[25] Particularly in Puritan spirituality, "self-emptying philanthropy," which includes both "denouncing greed, waste, and self-indulgence and serving the deprived, neglected, and suffering," was highlighted as proof of a Christian spiritual life.[26] This moral view of spirituality is still prominent in many contemporary Protestant churches.

Last, the Pentecostal and charismatic movements today demonstrate another type of Protestant spirituality. They understand Christian spirituality as a revitalization of life by means of such extraordinary experiences of the Holy Spirit as speaking in tongues, prophecies, and testimonies, as well as expressive body language in the form of raised hands, clapping, kneeling, and dancing. These physical manifestations are considered evidence of the presence and power of the Holy Spirit and significant factors in revitalizing the spirituality of the believers. Those who are suffering in the world from economic poverty, physical or mental illness, failure in business, psychological depression, or despair are convinced to overcome these predicaments by experiencing the charismatic power of the Spirit and are encouraged to cope with their suffering and hardship in this world.[27] In the sense that spirituality is an individual, inward experience of the Spirit, the charismatic understanding of Christian spirituality is consistent with Western mysticism, while its expression and practice are different.[28]

It is true that these mystical, moral, and charismatic understandings of spirituality co-exist in Asian American churches. However, they cannot represent an authentic Christian spirituality for Asian Americans because they do not embrace in balance the three characteristics of Asian American ethnic spirituality, namely, critical transcendence, spiritual sensibility, and the sense of communality. Rather, they have caused confusion in guiding the spiritual life of congregations. For Asian American Christians, to live in the Spirit is to live as a sign of what God in Christ is for. Likewise, spirituality means the ability to guide the congregation toward the holistic transformation of humanity beyond a reclusive or private experience of the divine. Therefore, Christian spirituality is not only descriptive but also prescriptive. It provides the congregation with a direction for their spiritual journey and at the same time helps them interpret their present condition from God's eschatological promise in Christ. This distinctive form of spirituality, which we will call Christian eschatological spirituality, can be explored further in relation to three doctrinal themes — the sovereignty of God, God the Holy Spirit, and the church as the nurturing community. Through these theological discussions, Asian American ethnic spirituality is transformed into Christian spirituality.

The Sovereignty of God

The critical point of transcendence in Asian spirituality occurs when one begins to realize that the sovereignty of God over the world holds the key to developing Asian American Christian spirituality.

Throughout Christian history, eschatology has been understood as the doctrine of the last things, emphasizing primarily the salvation of the individual's soul after death. However, the discovery of the significance of Christian apocalyptic eschatology in the Bible resituated eschatology in the center of Christian theology. Jürgen Moltmann acknowledges that "eschatology is not an appendix to dogmatic but an essential key to the unlocking of Christian truth" since apocalyptic eschatology provides the basic framework for understanding the structure and thought of the gospel.[29]

Christian apocalyptic eschatology is a transformed concept of Jewish apocalyptic eschatology, which focuses on the kingdom of God based on the dualistic worldview. Its main theme is the sovereignty of God in Jesus Christ, that is, the restoration of the lordship of Christ.[30] Jewish apocalyptic anticipates a radically different world not by the steady and continuous change of historical, political, and social conditions but by a cosmic catastrophe that will do away with all conditions of the present world. The struggle between the powers of good and evil, the universal reign of the one true God, and the message of comfort with hope and promise for the future to the faithful in their times of most bitter suffering are its major concerns.[31] The early church connected these future-oriented Jewish apocalyptic themes into their experience of Jesus of Nazareth and reinterpreted them in relation to christological events.

As Ernst Käsemann points out, the cross, resurrection, and second coming of Jesus Christ transformed the traditional Jewish concept of apocalypse into the Christian version.[32] The expectation of the future is now grounded in the promise of God, the second coming of Christ. The fulfillment of the second coming of Christ is already on its way by the first coming of Jesus Christ. The historical events of the cross and resurrection of Christ are "not a backward but a forward look toward the day of his coming again 'in power and in glory.'"[33] Likewise, future-oriented Jewish apocalyptic eschatology became proleptic in the Christian community after Easter. The kingdom of God is no longer a remote future but is already experienced by those Christians who confess Jesus as the Lord, although the future is yet to come. Even though Christians live in the unjust present world, the eschatological hope for the fulfillment of the universal sovereignty of God in Christ provides the essential meaning of their lives. Therefore, the fundamental concern of the Christian apocalyptic message is, To whom does the sovereignty of the world belong? Christian hope is based on the conviction that God is Lord of the world.[34]

The critical transcendence of Asian spirituality is based on the belief that the goal of humanity is to fulfill the will of heaven, which is the liberation of the oppressed. So Christian apocalyptic eschatology is based on the belief that "the ultimate victory is God's, who lives with people and gives them the power of truth, love, and justice." The former is rooted in the doctrine that humanity is a natural and essential aspect of human nature. The latter, by contrast, is grounded in God's promise in the second coming of Jesus Christ. The cross and resurrection of Christ Jesus are the source of Christian eschatological spirituality, since those christological events give us the power to cope with the present evil power in our suffering. Likewise, this eschatological framework provides Christian spirituality with a theological direction in the dialectical tension between the present reality and the future of God. In this proleptic time framework, Christian life is guided by the Holy Spirit, who points and directs us toward the future.

God the Holy Spirit

The spiritual sensibility of Asian spirituality leads Asian American churches to take seriously the presence and work of the Holy Spirit in daily lives. Asian Americans have realized culturally and religiously the presence and power of divine spirits and have experienced their influence on the transformation of human nature and society. Correspondingly, Christian eschatology is deeply related to the presence and work of the Holy Spirit. However, its understanding of the Spirit is far different from the traditional Asian concept.

In order to clarify the meaning of the Holy Spirit, it is necessary first to survey the prevailing view of the Holy Spirit within the Christian church. As Moltmann indicates in *The Spirit of Life*, Western theology has tended to understand the Holy Spirit not fully in the Trinitarian framework. That is, the Holy Spirit has been regarded not essentially as "consubstantial" with the Father and the Son but functionally as subordinate to them, lacking a distinctive place in the Trinity.[35] The Western tradition of *filioque*, which refers to the addition of "and from the Son" to the statement "the Holy Spirit proceeds from the Father"[36] reinforced the inferior position of the Spirit in the Trinity. This Western theological tendency has resulted in an imbalance in understanding the Trinitarian God both by emphasizing only the christological events in the New Testament as the center of Christian theology without relating to Christology to pneumatology and by ignoring the work of God as the Spirit in the Old Testament and in our contemporary lives.[37]

Under this influence, Western homiletics has placed preaching in the Christocentric view and has overlooked the nature and function of the Holy Spirit in relation to preaching. Centering on an intellectual acknowledgment of the doctrine of forgiveness in Jesus Christ by grace alone, Protestant homileticians have developed a christocentric theology of preaching.[38] Moreover, theological subordination of the

Trinity has led homileticians to misunderstand the relationship between the Holy Spirit and preaching. That is, just as the Spirit has
been regarded as the "mode of efficacy" in Western theology, relegat-
ing it to the role of handmaid to the Father and the Son, so Western
homiletics has understood the Spirit merely functionally, as aiding
in the delivery of a sermon. For example, John Broadus, in *On the
Preparation and Delivery of Sermons*, deals with the Holy Spirit briefly,
considering the Spirit to be an aid or support in the preparation and
delivery of preaching in order to make preaching more effective.[39]
Contemporary homiletics, whose major concern is the methodology
of rhetoric, is in most cases silent when discussing the role of the
Holy Spirit in preaching.[40] It seems to feel that the Spirit either conflicts with human rhetoric or is unnecessary in developing a method
of preaching.

By contrast, the theology of preaching that is concerned with
Christian eschatological spirituality understands the Holy Spirit in
relation to substance, that is, "the divine 'nature' (*phusis*), which is
fully and identically present as each of the three hypostases" of the
Trinity.[41] God is both one and three at the same time. This substan-
tial understanding of the Holy Spirit as one member of the Trinity
leads us to realize not merely that the Spirit is something God and
Christ possess but also that God is Spirit and has the Spirit at the
same time. The Holy Spirit is not an assistant to God the Father or
to Christ the Son but is related to them as a distinct person of the
same divine substance. God is in essence the Spirit, and in the mode
of the Spirit God dwells in, with, and among us continuously as our
companion who shares our suffering and hardship. So, we are never
apart from God. God is present among us through the Holy Spirit
in three ways — as the life-giving energy of life, as the sustainer of
our lives, and as the transforming force of the world. This threefold
aspect of the Holy Spirit is closely connected to Christian eschatological spirituality and plays a major role in the formation and nurture
of spirituality.

First, the Holy Spirit functions as life-giving energy. The Old and
New Testaments identify the nature of the Spirit with *ruach* in Hebrew and *pneuma* in Greek. These words are often translated "wind"
or "breath."[42] As "God is spirit" (John 4:24), God is also wind and

breath. God is a tempest, a storm, and a force penetrating all existing beings of God's creation in the universe. The Spirit experienced in us is the source of vitality to heal, to regenerate, and to sanctify our life.[43]

This life-giving energy carries out the consummation of God's eschatological promise in Christ. That is, the actualization of Christian hope for a new heaven and a new earth does not depend on what is possible and impossible in the realistic sense but on the power of the Spirit. Thus, Christians who believe in the presence and power of the Holy Spirit do not despair even if we see no positive evidence in the present moment; rather, we transcend present suffering since we believe through the Spirit that "the sufferings of this present time are not worth comparing with the glory about to be revealed to us" (Romans 8:18). Christian eschatological spirituality is built upon and nurtured in this faithful conviction.

It gives the meaning of life to the whole creation that "has been groaning in labor pains until now" (Romans 8:22). Therefore, the Holy Spirit as life-giving energy provides Christian spirituality with a point, purpose, and direction. Moltmann's affirmation of the significance of the doctrine of the Holy Spirit is valid:

> It is pneumatology that brings Christology and eschatology together. There is no mediation between Christ and the kingdom of God except the present experience of the Spirit, for the Spirit is the Spirit of Christ and the living energy of the new creation of all things. In the present of the Spirit are both origin and consummation.[44]

Second, the Holy Spirit functions as the sustainer of our lives. The Spirit is the Comforter (*paraclete*), Helper, or Advocate for us. The Spirit upholds believers so that they can be new beings and nourishes, protects, and consoles them while they are living in this world. Likewise, the Spirit as the sustainer has a feminine image, like a mother who cares for her children.[45] Jung Young Lee stresses this feminine image of the Holy Spirit when relating it to the Asian context: the image of God the Spirit as a gentle mother appeals to Asians more than that of a stern father. This is because the metaphor of father in Asian culture has been distorted by the image of the strict and stubborn patriarch of hierarchical Confucian society. The Holy Spirit can

be experienced intimately by Asian and Asian American Christians
if they see the Spirit as a mother who is always near her children
and maintains a close relationship with them. The image of an Asian
mother who willingly sacrifices herself for her children's sake also
aids in understanding the essence of God who died for us on the
cross.[46]

The experience of the Holy Spirit who is like a mother caring for
her children is a source of joy despite the suffering and hardships of
this world. Believers are not abandoned or alone but are already living in a new age in the nurture of the Holy Spirit. God acts through
the Spirit within our lives and "helps us in our weakness," says Paul,
"for we do not know how to pray as we ought, but that very Spirit
intercedes with sighs too deep for words. And God, who searches the
heart, knows what is the mind of the Spirit, because the Spirit intercedes for the saints according to the will of God" (Romans 8:26–27).
The Spirit, who is God the Mother, shares suffering and hardships
with her children and encourages them by reminding them of the
promise in Christ Jesus.

Although the present experience of the Spirit as God the Mother
does not mean the fulfillment of the future promise of God in the believer's life, it is significant because such an experience is a "foretoken"
of the kingdom of God for the assurance of the community's faith.
It convinces us that God in the mode of the Spirit always acts in the
world and makes an immediate impact on day-to-day human life. It
renews the promise of God and reaffirms our hope in God's promise.
In this sense, this spiritual experience can be called an "exhilarating
foretaste" of the kingdom of God.[47] Therefore, Christian spirituality based on the sustaining power of the Spirit is characterized as a
paradigmatic or parabolic power through which we grasp in advance
the reality of the restoration of the lordship of Christ. Through our
fragmentary experience of the kingdom of God in the Spirit, "we see
in a mirror, dimly" but anticipate the day when "we will see face to
face" (1 Corinthians 13:12).

Last, the Holy Spirit functions as the transforming force of the
world. When Paul the apostle described the Spirit as the life-giving
spirit of the risen Christ in 1 Corinthians 15:45, he meant the
Spirit as that which brings about the transformation of the world

with justice and righteousness. The Spirit is acting in order to establish "God's humanizing activity in the world,"[48] borrowing Paul
Lehmann's terminology. In other words, humans are creatures of God,
but they live as sinners by ignoring the call of God, which demands
a responsible answer. However, God's action through Jesus Christ has
provided them with the initiative for that humanization, that is, "to
live by faith" as believers.[49] Now, the Holy Spirit as a mode of the
presence of God reveals and guarantees God's transcendent power in
transforming all the human affairs of the world. When the Holy
Spirit breaks into the human spirit and drives it out of itself, the
human spirit is then transformed and transcendentally aligned with
God. The Spirit as a radical transforming divine power guides and
directs human life in order "to make and to keep human life human
in the world."[50]

The Holy Spirit as the transforming force is present in multi-
dimensions of human life: in the individual's daily life, in the
community of faith, in the specific situations of society, and in human
history and nature in general. It not only dwells in them but also
works for their radical transformation. That is, it works to establish
a new relationship between God and the world by renewing the individual, by vitalizing the community of faith, by directing the society,
which is waiting for a response from the church, and by restor-
ing God's creation, which encompasses the whole world. Therefore,
Christian spirituality that is sustained by this eschatological power of
the Spirit is not a static state but a dynamic movement of believers
who are called by the Spirit to participate in the politics of God, or
the politics of humanization. The Spirit continuously invites believers to participate in transforming self-justifying and self-perpetuating
worldly politics into the politics of God that restores the cosmic
lordship of Christ in every dimension of God's creation.[51]

Traditional concepts of spirituality include such subjective experiences as mystical moments of ecstasy, individual piety, or private
experiences of charismatic power. They need to be extended to
embrace the universal and holistic dimension of the presence and
work of the Spirit. Christian eschatological spirituality includes not
merely the personal dimension but also the sociopolitical and eco-
logical concerns inherent in society and in the world. Christian

eschatological spirituality is a special call from God to live a parabolic and paradigmatic life that represents the restored image of God in this world.

The Church as the Nurturing Community

Just as Asian spirituality is concerned primarily with communal well-being, so Christian eschatological spirituality is concerned with taking responsibility for the renewal of relationships with God and others in the community. It inspires a new vision for the Asian American community, an inclusive society in which different ethnic groups establish corporate relationships with one another for unity and harmony in society. This vision based on God's eschatological promise is not only a dream; it is to be realized by stimulating the congregation to cooperate in making that vision come true in society.

This community-centered spirituality cannot be nourished privately in a reclusive, solitary life but only in the community of faith. The church is the context for the formation and nurture of Christian eschatological spirituality. Here, the church signifies the *koinonia*. The *koinonia*, as Lehmann defines it in *Ethics in a Christian Context*, is neither identical with the visible church nor separate from it. It is the true church that can be understood by the metaphor of the body, or a new "fellowship-reality" between Jesus Christ and the believers.[52] It is "the fellowship-creating reality of Christ's presence in the world."[53] Fellowship means brotherly and sisterly love toward one another. It is not a social club organized to serve the members' interests but a community of self-sacrifice in which the members share their possessions, goods, time, energy, safety, and even their lives for the sake of one another.[54]

In this regard, the Asian perception of family can be helpful in understanding the nature of *koinonia*. In Asian and Asian American culture, the primary locus of human relationships is not the individual but the family. Self-fulfillment or cultivation of the individual begins with one's family and then expands to relationships with neighborhood, community, nation, and the cosmos.[55] By experiencing love and care in the family, the members build their own identity as a part of that one body and contribute to solidarity and shared responsibility for the family.

In turn, the *koinonia* as the body of Christ is the family and household of God.[56] The community of faith as an extended family is the place where believers identify themselves with that one body by sharing certain traditions and incorporating them into a common worldview. They share solidarity and responsibility as members of one body. Just as the Asian concept of human relationship begins with the family and expands to neighbor, society, nation, and the cosmos, so the world is the ultimate place where the believer lives in Spirit. The individual believer becomes new through fellowship with others in the body of Christ and expresses that newness toward the world as a living parable.

However, it is also important to note distinctions between the *koinonia* and the Asian family structure. First, while the family is bound by human blood ties or family connections, the *koinonia* is formed by a call to the eschatological community, the covenantal bond between God and the believers. Second, the *koinonia* is created by the christological events. Jesus' cross and resurrection, which were historical events, now justify the members of the church, while his second coming places the church in the category of a parabolic power.[57] In this sense, the church as the *koinonia* exists as a fragmentary and anticipatory reality within the limits of time and space. It is a community that participates in the creation of new beings, a new society, and a new world anticipating the future fulfillment of God's promise.

Therefore, Asian American spirituality that is rooted in God's promise takes seriously the function of the church. The Asian American church is the locus where their rich spiritual and cultural heritage meets the Christian message and then is synthesized to form the communal identity. This nurtures the congregation's spiritual life with a Christian identity by means of new images and stories created from the reinterpretation of the Asian cultural tradition in light of the liberating Word of God. Each member is called to a concrete vocational situation and to assume responsibilities in society as a living parable. In this manner, Christian eschatological spirituality transforms the corporate personality of the community of faith into a subversive power for the transformation of the world.

Spiritual Preaching

Preaching based on Christian eschatological spirituality is called spiritual preaching. Its primary goal is the formation and nurture of the congregation's spirituality. Its nature and function and the image and role of the preacher for spiritual preaching can be explained as follows.

The Nature of Preaching

Spiritual preaching is based on the theological conviction that God the Spirit was, is, and will be present among the congregation and has been revealed to them through preaching. Thus, it anticipates the presence of the Holy Spirit at the moment of preaching. If the Spirit is not present in preaching, then the sermon is the mere expression of an idea with no power to grip the listeners. But when the Holy Spirit is present, human words become the Word of God and preaching becomes spiritual, with the power to invade, transform, and elevate the listeners' spirits.

The experience of the Holy Spirit in preaching is not merely individual but also communal. That is, it is a group experience of unity and harmony in the Spirit beyond a private inward experience of soul. Through preaching, the listeners share a common feeling that Christ is in them all, that they are one in Christ, loved by and trusting in God. This is a holistic and inspirational experience of the divine. In this sense, whereas the Eucharist is a visible communal meal, spiritual preaching is an invisible communal meal that nourishes the community of faith spiritually.

Spiritual preaching that is holistic and inspirational is enhanced when it is integrated with other liturgical elements in the service of worship. Prayers and hymns, confession and pardon, the affirmation of faith, anthems and Scripture readings, baptism and Eucharist, charge and blessing cooperate with preaching to bring about a sense of God's presence in the service. They lead the congregation to open themselves to feel the presence of God, to be gripped by the power of the Holy Spirit, and to be voluntarily changed. When the congregation encounters the Holy Spirit beyond a limited human domain through preaching, they not only realize something new in the Bible intellectually but also are emotionally touched, intuitively enlightened, and voluntarily moved.

If preaching becomes the moment of experiencing the presence of the living God, it is God's gift for two reasons. For one, it is because we humans can experience God only when God opens God's self to us. The preacher cannot bring about an experience of the holy divine Spirit by human efforts alone but is dependent on God's self-revelation. As Barth says: "As ministers we ought to speak of God. We are human, however, and so cannot speak of God. We ought therefore to recognize our obligation and our inability and by that very recognition give God the glory."[58] For another reason, it is because God uses preaching as a medium of self-disclosure. Through human rhetoric in preaching, God accommodates the various situations and capacities of the congregation. The preacher's rhetorical approach to biblical interpretation, sermonic form and language, and delivery participates in the revelation of God. At the same time, the congregation's willingness to experience the Word of God is one of the most significant factors for making the truth come alive among them.

Therefore, spiritual preaching as an experience of the living God is possible only by relying on God's gracious partnership with humans. In this regard, the authority of preaching is understood from God's side rather than the human side. Such external qualities as a preacher's gender, age, educational level, or social position cannot be the source of that authority because it originates not from any human standard but from God's grace.

The Function of Preaching

Spiritual preaching functions as a fragmentary foretaste of the messianic feast in three ways. First, it helps the congregation to visualize itself in the promise of God. By critically reflecting on the reality of the congregation from the perspective of God's humanizing activity, it describes a new world in which people enjoy their restored relationship with God and with others. It does not ignore the present suffering and experience of the congregation but rather acknowledges them and promises a hopeful horizon beyond their current state. A vision for the community includes the future of the individual, society, and nature as they await the consummation of God's salvation as an integrated whole of God's creation. Just as God's humanizing activity penetrates all dimensions of creation, so the dimension of the content of spiritual preaching includes God's entire creation.

Second, spiritual preaching invites the listeners to participate in the politics of God. Those who see the vision for the community of faith look at the world in a different way than ever before. They then live out what they see because the vision relativizes the existing reality of the world; it warns the oppressors of the judgment of God and offers comfort and hope to the oppressed. It also admonishes those wavering between dedication to God's order and trust in human ideologies. Therefore, people who listen to spiritual preaching no longer support the human politics of the established order or the world's standards of materialism, classism, racism, and sexism. Their lives are now distinguished from such a life in the world. Those who experience the living God through preaching are filled with joy in God's promise and are inspired by a desire to take responsibility for the humanization of the world.

Third, spiritual preaching engages the listeners at an ethical level. Here, Lehmann helps distinguish ethics from morality: While morality is a practice or behavior according to custom, ethics is a "reflection upon the foundations and principles of behavior."[59] The primary concern of spiritual preaching is not a moralistic exhortation but the will of God. Morality is the byproduct of spiritual maturity. Spiritual preaching guides the congregation by allowing them to reflect on their lives ethically. Its approach is not imperative, instructing the listeners to "Do this!" by giving some moral principles or rules for what they must do. Instead it is fundamentally indicative as the eschatological vision is indicative. It directs the listeners to reflect Who am I? and calls them to be mature in Jesus Christ as living parables of God's promise to the world.[60]

Therefore, the goal of spiritual preaching is political in the sense that it seeks to form an alternative community by invoking the Holy Spirit to guide the corporate personality of the community toward eschatological spirituality. It aims to build a new community, the *koinonia*, as an agent of God's politics for the transformation of the world. Spiritual preaching, as a spiritual meal, contributes to the formation and nurture of the congregation's spirituality.

The Image of the Preacher

The preacher of spiritual preaching serves as director of the congregation's spiritual life. The preacher as spiritual director is neither a miracle worker sweeping away the listeners' problems nor a heavenly herald declaring the holy will of the divine nor a sage passing his or her knowledge and wisdom to the followers. Rather, the preacher is a mediator giving direction to their spiritual life by helping them experience the presence and power of God the Spirit in their lives.

The authority of the preacher mediating between the congregation and God comes both from the call of God to be a coworker of God's enterprise and from the call of the congregation to be a disciplined spiritual leader to give them guidance on their spiritual journey. It means that God calls the preacher in order to reveal God's presence through human words, and the congregation needs someone to share their life journey as a "co-pilgrim,"[61] to listen to them, affirm them, and help them clarify their thoughts and feelings by exploring the Scriptures in a communal context.

Through a shared journey over time with the congregation, the preacher dreams of a radically new world as an alternative for the present community and anticipates the realization of this vision within the community. At this point, the preacher as spiritual director is both dreamer and politician. By revealing to the listeners things that they have hitherto been unable to see, the preacher strengthens them to live as a living parable of God in the world. This vision arises from a conversation between the biblical text and the contemporary experience of the listeners. A vision created by listening to individuals and then discovering mutual affinities and similarities transforms the congregation's corporate personality as well as individual personalities and redirects their spirituality with an eschatological orientation. This vision nourishes the congregation with faith, hope, and love and leads them to participate in the politics of God for a unified and harmonious future in the promise of God.

In this regard, the task of the preacher as spiritual director is to provide the community of faith with a visionary sermon, a spiritual meal, week after week. Like a traditional Asian mother who lovingly prepares a dinner with nutritious food according to the family's taste and needs, so the preacher prepares a sermon as a weekly spiritual meal for the congregation. This analogy can help preachers understand the process of preparation for preaching.

First, just as a mother prepares a meal with love and concern for the family, so the preacher begins the preparation for preaching with love and concern for the congregation. Second, just as the mother does her meal planning for some period of time, so the preacher needs to make a preaching plan. Whether it is based on the lectionary or the local church calendar or the preacher's own plan, it should be balanced theologically and spiritually. Third, fresh ingredients make the food savory and nutritious. Likewise, choosing a text and giving it new meaning on the basis of the particular experience of the congregation are essential to preparing for spiritual preaching. Fourth, such diverse cooking methods as steaming, boiling, grilling, or frying and the use of various sauces or special spices allow a variety of dishes to emerge. For example, with tomato sauce food becomes Italian; with curry, Indian; with soy sauce and cornstarch, Chinese; and with red pepper and sesame oil, Korean. Likewise, sermons become diverse by adopting diverse sermonic forms and seasoning with various cultural additions and expressions. Fifth, the cooked food needs to be placed in the right container. Soup cannot be carried on a flat plate. A roasted turkey requires a platter, not a small bowl. In the same way, a sermon needs a proper delivery to carry the message effectively. Finally, at the dinner table, the plate should complement the other elements of the meal for a joyful mood at mealtime. Likewise, preaching is integrated with other liturgical elements in worship. The preacher as spiritual director provides the communal meal for the nourishment of the congregation's spiritual growth and mediates on behalf of the congregation to draw forth the fruits of the Holy Spirit — love, joy, peace, patience, kindness, generosity, faithfulness, gentleness, and self-control (Galatians 5:22–23).

Conclusion

The theology of Asian American preaching is closely related to the formation and nurture of the congregation's spirituality. Spiritual preaching based on Christian eschatological spirituality is concerned with guiding the community of faith with a vision for the future of the community. It helps the listeners experience the living God through dialogue, inquiry, and response between the biblical text and their experience. It aims to develop Christian identity within the community of faith and reorients its corporate personality toward God's promise. The preacher as spiritual director serves the congregation by guiding the way along their spiritual journey and by encouraging their participation in the politics of God with a vision for the kingdom of God.

In spiritual preaching, human rhetoric is a vehicle for God's self-revelation. All components of preaching such as content, form, language, and delivery are concerned with how to invite listeners to experience the presence and power of the Holy Spirit in their lives. Therefore, another task of the Asian American homiletic is to develop rhetorical devices for the fulfillment of that goal. The following chapters will concentrate on methodological issues in relation to the method of biblical interpretation, the design of sermonic form, and the use of language.

Notes

1. See Sang Hyun Lee, "Asian-American Theology: 'Called to be Pilgrims,'" in *Korean American Ministry*, ed. Sang Hyun Lee and John V. Moore (Louisville: General Assembly Council, PCUSA, 1987), 39–65.

2. Kenneth J. Collins, "What Is Spirituality? Historical and Methodological Consideration," *Wesleyan Theological Journal* 31 (spring 1996): 77–78.

3. Young-Hak Hyun, "Minjung the Suffering Servant and Hope," in *Essays on Korean Heritage and Christianity*, ed. Sang Hyun Lee (Princeton Junction, N.J.: The Association of Korean Christian Scholars in North America, 1984), 47.

4. Young-Hak Hyun, "A Theological Look at the Mask Dance in

Korea," in *Minjung Theology: People as the Subjects of History*, ed. Yong Bok Kim (Singapore: The Commission on Theological Concern of the Christian Conference of Asia, 1981), quoted from David Kwang-sun Suh, "Minjung Theology: The Politics and Spirituality of Korean Christianity," in *Perspectives on Christianity in Korea and Japan: The Gospel and Culture in East Asia*, ed. Mark R. Mullins and Richard Fox Young (Lewiston, N.Y.: Edwin Mellen Press, 1995), 151.

5. Suh.

6. Hyun, "Minjung the Suffering Servant and Hope," 42–46.

7. C. S. Song, *The Tears of Lady Meng: A Parable of People's Political Theology* (Geneva: World Council of Churches, 1981), 1–20.

8. Ibid., 44–66.

9. Hector Diaz, *A Korean Theology: Chu-Gyo Yo-Ji = Essentials of the Lord's Teaching, by Chong Yak-jong Augustine (1760–1801)* (Immensee: Neue Zeitschrift fur Missionswissenschaft, 1986), 203–4.

10. Ibid., 123.

11. Muneo J. Yoshikawa, "Japanese and American Modes of Communication and Implications for Managerial and Organizational Behavior," a paper presented at the Second International Conference on Communication Theory from Eastern and Western Perspectives (July 1982): 23–25.

12. Arthur Waley, trans., *The Analects of Confucius* (New York: Vintage, 1989), 30.

13. Young-chan Ro, *The Korean Neo-Confucianism of Yi Yolgok* (New York: State University of New York Press, 1988), 87.

14. Waley, 88–89.

15. Robert E. Kennedy, *Zen Spirit, Christian Spirit* (New York: Continuum, 1996), 26; Hajime Nakamura, *Ways of Thinking of Eastern Peoples: India, China, Tibet, Japan* (Honolulu: East-West Center Press, 1964), 251–52.

16. Ronald Y. Nakasone, *Ethics of Enlightenment: Essays and Sermons in Search of a Buddhist Ethic* (Fremont, Calif.: Dharma Cloud Publishers, 1990), 97.

17. June-Ock Yum, "Korean Philosophy and Communication," in *Communication Theory*, ed. D. Lawrence Kincaid (San Diego: Academic Press, 1987), 81.

18. Chung Hyun Kyung, *Struggle to Be the Sun Again: Introducing Asian Women's Theology* (Maryknoll, N.Y.: Orbis, 1990), 112.

19. David K. Suh, *The Korean Minjung in Christ* (Kowloon, Hong Kong: The Christian Conference of Asia: Commission on Theological Concerns, 1991), 100.

20. See L. Bouyer, *The Spirituality of the New Testament and the Fathers*, vol. 1 of *A History of Christian Spirituality* (New York: Seabury, 1982); *The Desert Fathers on Monastic Community* (Oxford: Clarendon, 1993).

21. See Giles Constable, *Medieval Monasticism: A Selected Bibliography* (Toronto: University of Toronto Press, 1976).

22. See Thomas Merton, *Spiritual Direction and Meditation and What Is Contemplation?* (Wheathampstead: A. Clarke, 1975); F. K. Nemeck, O.M.I., and Marie Theresa Coombs, Hermit, *The Way of Spiritual Direction* (Wilmington, Del.: Michael Glazier, 1985); Juel S. Goldsmith, *The Art of Meditation* (New York: Harper, 1956).

23. Collins, 80–81.

24. Ibid., 81; see also Lucien J. Richard, *The Spirituality of John Calvin* (Atlanta: John Knox, 1974).

25. Louis Dupré and Don E. Saliers, eds., *Christian Spirituality: Post-Reformation and Modern* (New York: Crossroad, 1989), 339–43; Irvonwy Morgan, *Puritan Spirituality* (London: Epworth, 1973).

26. Dupré and Saliers, 242–46.

27. See Harvey Cox, *Fire from Heaven: The Rise of Pentecostal Spirituality and the Reshaping of Religion in the Twenty-first Century* (Reading, Mass.: Addison-Wesley, 1995).

28. Jürgen Moltmann, *The Spirit of Life* (Minneapolis: Fortress, 1992), 185–86.

29. Jürgen Moltmann, *Theology of Hope* (San Francisco: Harper, 1991 [German, 1965]), 40.

30. Ernst Käsemann, "The Beginning of Christian Theology," in *New Testament Questions of Today* (Philadelphia: Fortress, 1979 [German, 1965]), 105.

31. Paul Hanson, *Old Testament Apocalyptic* (Nashville: Abingdon, 1987), 34.

32. Käsemann, 105.

33. Paul Lehmann, "Editorial — Evanston: Problems and Prospects," *Theology Today* 11, no. 2 (July 1954): 149.

34. Ernst Käsemann, "On the Subject of Primitive Christian Apocalyptic," in *New Testament Questions of Today* (Philadelphia: Fortress, 1979 [German, 1965]), 135.

35. Moltmann, *Spirit of Life*, 1.

36. Everett Ferguson, ed., *Encyclopedia of Early Christianity* (New York and London: Garland, 1990), 347.

37. Moltmann, *Spirit of Life*, 8.

38. See Karl Barth, *Homiletics*, trans. Geoffrey W. Bromiley and Donald E. Daniels (Louisville: Westminster/John Knox, 1991); John Knox, *The Integrity of Preaching* (New York: Abingdon, 1957).

39. John Broadus, *On the Preparation and Delivery of Sermons*, rev. Vernon L. Standfield (San Francisco: Harper, 1979), 16–17.

40. For example, see H. Grady Davis, *Design for Preaching* (Philadelphia: Muhlenberg, 1958).

41. Ferguson, 872.

42. For example, Genesis 2:7; Job 27:3; Isaiah 42:5; John 3:8; Acts 2:2.

43. Jung Young Lee, *The Trinity in Asian Perspective* (Nashville: Abingdon, 1996), 96.

44. Moltmann, *Spirit of Life*, 69.

45. For example, John 14:17,26; 15:26; 16:8–11,13.

46. Lee, *The Trinity in Asian Perspective*, 105.

47. Paul Lehmann, *Ethics in a Christian Context* (New York: Harper & Row, 1963), 123.

48. Ibid., 357.

49. Paul Lehmann, "Man as Believer," *The Journal of Religious Thought* 2, no. 2 (1945): 179; Romans 1:17; cf. Romans 5:1–5.

50. Paul Lehmann, *The Transfiguration of Politics* (New York: Harper & Row, 1975), 85; Paul Tillich, *Systematic Theology*, vol. 3 (Chicago: University of Chicago Press, 1976), 111–12.

51. Lehmann, *The Transfiguration of Politics*, 20.

52. Lehmann, *Ethics in a Christian Context*, 47.

53. Ibid., 49.

54. Ibid., 50.

55. Heup Young Kim and David Ng, "The Central Issue of Community," in *People on the Way: Asian North Americans Discovering Christ, Culture, and Community*, ed. David Ng (Valley Forge, Pa.: Judson, 1996), 32.

56. Ibid., 39.

57. Lehmann, *Ethics in a Christian Context*, 45.

58. Karl Barth, "The Word of God and the Task of the Ministry," in *The Word of God and the Word of Man* (Gloucester, Mass.: Peter Smith, 1978), 186.

59. Lehmann, *Ethics in a Christian Context*, 24–25.

60. Ibid., 54–55.

61. John Westerhoff, *Spiritual Life: The Foundation for Preaching and Teaching* (Louisville: Westminster/John Knox, 1994), 48.

Chapter Three

A Hermeneutic

Since the Bible is a product of multiple authors from different traditional, geographical, linguistic, and cultural backgrounds, it is necessary to devise a systematic plan for understanding the deeper meaning of the text for preaching. Through a process of interpretation, the message of God's promise in the Bible is relevant to the context of the congregation in guiding them along their spiritual journey. Therefore, Asian American preaching, which concerns itself with Christian eschatological spirituality and with the congregation's particular cultural orientation, requires of the preacher a special hermeneutical discipline.

The term *hermeneutics* is heard frequently in the fields of biblical studies, philosophy, aesthetics, and literary criticism. It has been variously defined, encompassing notions of translation, exegesis, modern theories of interpretation, and understanding human existence. This chapter conceives it as being concerned with establishing both a relevant view of the Bible and a systematic process of its interpretation. With this meaning, hermeneutics is by no means limited to Christian texts. In East Asia, Confucianism and Buddhism have developed particular hermeneutical methods based on their unique histories of canonization and views of the scriptures. Although little attention has been paid to them in developing Christian hermeneutics, it seems that their perspectives are promising in arriving at a particular method of biblical interpretation for Asian American congregations. They will complement theories of Christian hermeneutics and furthermore contribute to creating a new hermeneutical perspective for Asian American preaching.

Therefore, this chapter includes three phases in order to arrive at the formation of a hermeneutic for Asian American preaching. First

77

is an introduction of Confucian and Buddhist hermeneutics; second, an exploration of hermeneutical implications for preaching through dialogue between Asian and Western hermeneutics; third, the development of a spiritual hermeneutic based on that dialogue. This will better enable preaching to be the medium through which the congregation's spirituality is formed and nurtured.

Asian Hermeneutics

Confucian and Buddhist scriptures have long existed in China, Korea, and Japan. Before the Christian Bible was introduced to these East Asian countries, these earlier writings were read, explored, and interpreted in certain ways and had their authority within the communities as the Sacred Books. Although the scriptures of these two religions have different origins and different canonical processes, they were both believed to be revelations of truth and were used as the medium for guiding individual and communal lives. The existence of these scriptures in East Asia paved the way for understanding the Christian Bible when it was later introduced. It was treated with the reverence accorded these traditional scriptures and contributed to guiding the spiritual lives of Asians.

It is not legitimate, however, to say that any particular Confucian or Buddhist tradition has a single hermeneutical method or only one underlying hermeneutical concern. There is no Confucian or Buddhist hermeneutic. Instead, we find a variety of approaches at different levels. This section attempts to present only a general understanding of Asian hermeneutics by examining Confucian and Buddhist ways of seeing the role of scriptures and their interpretive methods, hoping not to distort the greater tradition of Asian hermeneutics.

The Confucian View

In Confucianism, the scriptures are a collection of writings by sages who thoroughly understood or penetrated the way of humanity. Before Confucius, there were selections of literary works that recorded the deeds of the sages, the early rulers of Chinese antiquity. These were called classics and had perennial value from generation to generation as they exemplified the way of life. Among many groups of classics, the Five Classics, which were supposed to be the record of the early Chou period, were the most essential. These included the Book of Changes, the Book of Poetry, the Book of History, the Book of Rites, and Spring and Autumn Annals. Confucius and Mencius used this literature in their teaching as an aid in supporting their ideology. They interpreted these Classics in relation to their particular historical and political context in order to give people humane, moral principles. Neo-Confucianism, which has dominated East Asian society from the eleventh century to the present, reaffirmed the basic teachings of Confucius and Mencius. Chu Hsi, a Neo-Confucian scholar, added the Four Books — the Analects, the Book of Mencius, the Great Learning, and the Doctrine of the Mean — to the Confucian scriptures, claiming that they were the proper interpretive tools with which to approach the Five Classics. Since then, the Four Books and the Five Classics have become the official standard scriptures of Confucianism.[1]

Chu Hsi emphasizes the authority of the classics in terms of their function. He says that "we make use of the Classics only to understand principle. If principles are understood, we do not have to depend upon them." As a collection of writings "containing principle, *li*, the underlying moral nature immanent in the phenomenal world," they provide "solid and pragmatic teachings for the ethical and religious growth of the individual as well as the implementation of the individual's moral nature into the daily affairs of the world."[2] Therefore, Confucian classics function as guide books for the way of humanity. They serve as a medium for learning and self-cultivation. When the reader understands the principle of humanity, the medium itself becomes unnecessary.

In Neo-Confucian hermeneutics, the interpretive process has been generally practiced in three stages.[3] First is to read the surface meaning of the text. By analyzing its literary style and general tone and semantics, the interpreter understands its literal sense and sees the text in relation to a larger context. Second, the interpreter reviews commentaries in order to know how the text has been interpreted by other Confucian scholars. By referring to a range of interpretations from various historical contexts, the interpreter realizes the diversity of meaning within the text and does not stick rigidly to one meaning. The last stage is to cultivate a new meaning for the text in the contemporary context through meditation. The interpreter connects text and context through an "analogical projection" based on the belief that "things are distinct yet not fundamentally different from each other because they share the same *tao*."[4] Through this process, the interpreter attempts to discover "a lesson in moral or spiritual self-cultivation" beyond the literal sense of the text by internalizing the text through meditation.

Quiet-sitting, repetition and memorization of the text, and calligraphy are recommended as means of meditation. Remembering Chu Hsi's instruction, "A half-day of quiet-sitting, a half-day of study," Rodney L. Taylor explains that the Chu Hsi school favored the Buddhist meditation of quiet-sitting as a form of practice through which the reader could penetrate to the very core of his or her nature and develop self-cultivation.[5] In addition to quiet-sitting, repetition and memorization are considered important meditative tools. Chu Hsi also says that "in reading a book, one should recite it silently. Often excellent thoughts will come to him at midnight or while he is sitting in meditation. If one does not remember what he reads, his thoughts will not arise. After one has thoroughly understood the great foundation of a book, however, it will be easy to remember."[6]

Moreover, calligraphy is highly valued in Confucian meditation. This is not simply a practice of copying passages or phrases from the scriptures for their memorization but "a direct means to deep and profound understanding of the wisdom of the Classics or other sources and the reflection of such wisdom in the gradually developing moral nature of the individual."[7] During this practice, the reader is supposed to cultivate a moral and spiritual sense of the text by means of intuitive imagination.

Considering that many Asian American sermons readily apply the literal sense of the text to the listeners' moral life without profound philosophical or spiritual reflection, this threefold Confucian hermeneutics suggests how to interpret the text in a deeper way through meditation, thereby reaching the ultimate truth beyond its surface meaning.

The Buddhist View

Buddhist scriptures have a long and complicated process of can-onization. The Pali canon was the earliest collection of Buddha's teachings and was compiled based on his disciples' memorization and recitation more than a century after his death.[8] Mahayana Bud-dhism, which spread throughout East Asia, expanded the collection of scriptures by adding numerous new writings and commentaries of texts written by monks and nuns. It contained new religious and philosophical concepts, claiming that they revealed a truth taught by Buddha but concealed by "advanced" disciples until the proper time for their unveiling. This canonical process continued until the thirteenth century.[9]

In early Mahayana Buddhism, the scriptures were regarded as sacred books in the sense that they were identified with Buddha him-self or "the teachers of future generations in the same sense that Sakyamuni was the teacher of his contemporaries." However, when Mahayana Buddhism was introduced to China, these sacred or mys-tical characters of scripture were less emphasized due to the influence of indigenous Confucianism. Instead, the Buddhist scriptures were understood functionally in the sense that "unless the meaning of the words is grasped in everyday experience, the words remain a dead thing." More precisely speaking, the Buddha was understood to be like Confucius, a great sage whose teaching benefitted and trans-formed the human world, and scripture like a sort of Confucian Classic that carries normative teaching for humanity.[10]

This pragmatic view is climaxed in Zen Buddhism. Zen Buddhists understand the scriptures to be not merely the transmitted words of Buddha's teaching but the words "conveying the truths one needs for successful practice toward enlightenment."[11] For them, scripture is useful only insofar as it functions to further the immediate percep-tion of truth transcending the words.[12] This is possible only when the words in the scriptures function as a "live-word" removing all types of wrong knowledge and wrong conceptualization and leading the be-liever to experience personal liberation.[13] In this sense, the scriptures are a vehicle for reaching enlightenment, embodying and providing a direct means of access to the ultimate truth that the Buddha reached.

Their function is not merely to help the believer's cognitive understanding of truth but also to reach the stage of enlightenment, of new
being, of sage or Buddha or, in a Christian sense, of a new creation
in the Holy Spirit.

Based on this understanding, Buddhism, particularly Mahayana
Buddhism, emphasizes the study of scripture as a direct means of
access to Buddha's knowledge, wisdom, and supernatural powers. In
Perfection of Wisdom in Eight Thousand Lines, Sakyamuni Buddha encourages his disciple Ananda to study the scriptures thoroughly by
saying that

> I entrust and transmit to you this perfection of wisdom, laid out in
> letters, so that it may be available for learning, for bearing in mind,
> preaching, studying and spreading wide.... You should attend well to
> this perfection of wisdom, bear it well in mind, study it well, and
> spread it well. And when one learns it, one should carefully ana-
> lyze it grammatically, letter by letter, syllable by syllable, word by
> word.[14]

Learned monks and nuns are regarded as truly qualified to expound
on the texts and are allowed to give a series of lectures periodically on
a given text in the *sangha*, the Buddhist communities or monasteries.
They usually take a commentarial form much like the *lectio continua*
and interpret the book from beginning to end. Their preaching is
identified with teaching and their sermons with lectures.[15]

Zen and Pure Land, which are the main branches of Mahayana
Buddhism, agree on the fact that "the truth is transmitted not through
words or intelligence or cognitive understanding alone, but from an
enlightened mind to a mind capable of insight."[16] In order to reach
the moment of enlightenment, Pure Land Buddhism practices memorization, copying, or recitation of the text while Zen Buddhism
depends on intuitive meditation by reflecting on some words from
scripture.[17]

In relation to Zen hermeneutics, Daisetz T. Suzuki explains that
there are two ways of understanding — the analytic (*vijnana*) and
the intuitive (*prajna*). While the former divides and dissects reality into subject and object, the latter grasps reality in its oneness.
Here, intuition does not mean an ordinary instinctive sensibility but
is *sui generis*, which can be developed by spiritual discipline.[18] If a

flower is understood in an analytic way, the flower becomes a collection of pieces of petals, pollen, stamen, and stalk or is analyzed according to its components, such as hydrogen and oxygen. By contrast, intuitive understanding sees the flower as a whole that represents the universe itself.[19] The goal of Buddhist meditation is to reach this intuitive understanding of things beyond the analytic. Christmas Humphreys sees the process of intuitive understanding as a threefold spiral cycle:

> There is a Japanese saying to the effect that in the beginning a man sees mountains as mountains, and trees as trees; later, the mountains are no longer seen as mountains nor the trees as trees; later still, he sees once more the mountains to be mountains, and the trees as trees. In this analogy, an interesting schedule might be made of the mental cycle, constantly repeated, by which the indwelling consciousness, *vinnana*, moves from an early state through an "opposite," intermediate state to a "final" state, which, seen as a higher third above the two, is in fact the first with so much added experience.[20]

Through intuitive understanding, Buddhist hermeneutics goes beyond literal and scientific understanding toward a synthesized, integral realization of the object.

The examination of Confucian and Buddhist hermeneutics reveals that both view the authority of scriptures in a functional way. The scriptures are authoritative because they help the believers understand humanity or experience enlightenment. They are mediums for guiding the spiritual life of the believers to the truth. This view gives insight into understanding the authority of the Bible in relation to its function of guiding the spiritual life of the community of faith. Confucian and Buddhist hermeneutics also use meditation in common as the primary tool for interpretation. Here, meditation means a spiritual process of cultivating the vast potential of the mind beyond the limitations imposed by internal and external human circumstances. Their interpretive process based on meditation leads us to reevaluate the significance of meditation in the process of biblical interpretation. Meditation as a life-living relationship with God helps us to see the world critically and leads us to respond to reality from a profound biblical perspective.

Homiletical Implications

It is hard to imagine Christian preaching without its correlative biblical text. As the norm of Christian life and theology, the Bible's authority can be neither denied nor compromised as long as the preacher approaches the Bible as the text of a sermon through which the Word of God is to be proclaimed. The biblical text requires of the preacher strenuous efforts to deepen the understanding of the text in the particular context of the congregation. In the process of biblical interpretation, the preacher encounters two worlds, the world of the text and the world of the congregation, and then aims to connect them in order to create a new meaning for the sermon.

In what sense, then, is the Bible authoritative for preaching? What kind of interpretive method is effective for preaching to be spiritual? Protestant churches include various views of the Bible and have practiced diverse approaches to understand meaning of the text according to diverse denominational backgrounds, particular characteristics of local congregations, and the preacher's theological training.

These hermeneutical views will now be reevaluated from the Asian hermeneutical perspective as it relates to the understanding of the authority of the scriptures and the method of interpretation. This critical discussion will suggest some hermeneutical implications for developing a hermeneutic of Asian American preaching.

The Authority of the Bible

Traditional Calvinists and contemporary fundamentalists understand the Bible to be the Word of God on the basis of its infallibility. They regard the Bible as a collection of ahistorical and dogmatic statements about God. Using 2 Timothy 3:16, 2 Peter 1:19–21, and other texts as proof texts, they insist that verbal inspiration and the literal inerrancy of the Bible are the source of its authority.[21] The Bible contains perennial values and timeless principles for moral discernment. Therefore, for them, the Bible is authoritative because it "not only communicates the Word of God but is the Word of God."[22] The preacher often tends to be the mouthpiece of God by repeating biblical words or concepts with little attention to the historical context of the text. In order to gain meaning from the text for preaching, the preacher either transfers the description of the historical people of the text into a prescription for contemporary listeners or uses the text as a proof text supporting the preacher's personal morality or philosophy.

This approach is easily seen in many Asian American churches whose theological trend is fundamentalist. However, this premodern view, which does not reflect on the critical, rational investigation of the Bible, cannot become the paradigm of Asian American homiletic because it keeps the preacher from fully engaging or deeply reflecting on the biblical text from the contemporary listeners' context. Instead, the text is often read superficially, taken out of historical context merely to confirm the preacher's ideology, and misused to defend the preacher's personal thoughts based on his or her experience.

Since the Enlightenment, biblical scholars have doubted this premodern understanding of the authority of the Bible and challenged traditional Christianity as the object of that doubt. They have represented a massive theological break with traditional Christianity on the basis of human rationality and experience. For them, the Bible is no longer a timeless sacred book or an absolute norm that represents unconditional truth or guidelines for Christian life but is rather the historical heritage of the community of faith. They understand the authority of the Bible on the basis of its "historical factualness." The Bible is regarded as a collection of the historical religious documents of Judaism and Christianity and as the Judeo-Christian literature of the Greco-Roman world.[23] The goal of biblical interpretation is to discover the author's intention "behind the text" by means of such objective historical-critical methods as textual criticism, grammatical criticism, form criticism, redaction criticism, structuralism, and literary criticism. These are the major tools with which to investigate the meaning of the text at the time it was written for the original audience.

This modern historical view was so revolutionary that it ushered in a paradigm shift in the field of traditional biblical interpretation. However, this is not enough for it to be the model for Asian American preaching because this historical view of the Bible separates the meaning of the text from the contemporary context for preaching. In this perspective, the preacher as interpreter becomes a historian whose task is to provide the listeners with accurate information about the text, focusing on a historical and literary inquiry of the text.[24] Without ignoring the text's historical character, Asian American preaching is concerned with determining what it means for the congregation. At this point, Asian American preaching is challenged to search for an alternative view of the Bible.

It is notable that Karl Barth in his *Church Dogmatics* attempts to overcome the dilemma of the historical view of the Bible by emphasizing the canonical character of the Bible. According to him, the Bible is authoritative because it is not merely "a historical monument but rather [church] document, written proclamation."[25] Historical-critical scholarship can help the preacher to make a correct exposition of the text. But the real meaning of the text emerges in relation to the life of the church. The Bible as "the prophetic and apostolic word" provides the church with the norm of living to be the apostolic succession. It is "constantly exposed to absorption into the life, thought and utterance of the [church] inasmuch as it continually seeks to be understood afresh and hence expounded and interpreted."[26]

Barth's functional approach to the Bible as canon is consistent with the views of Brevard Childs, James Sanders, and David Kelsey. They understand in common that the Bible is the canon of the church. Here, canon means a set of writings developed through a historical process of selection by the Christian communities in order to be used in certain ways for shaping and nurturing their self-identity.[27] In this sense, Kelsey explains, the Bible as the canon of the community of faith functions to shape and preserve "both corporate identity as an integral community, and the personal identities of the individuals that make up the community."[28]

What, then, gives the Bible its canonical status? Barth says that it is the christological content of the Bible, that is, "the word, witness, proclamation and preaching of Jesus Christ."[29] The Bible is "the [church's] recollection of God's past revelation" in Jesus Christ.[30] It not only bears witness to the incarnation of the eternal Word and the reconciliation accomplished in the events of Jesus Christ but also promises the church a future revelation that has yet to come through him.[31] Rudolf Bultmann is party to the consensus view that the authoritative elements of the Bible are its christological statements, the kerygma. He contends that "Christian faith did not exist until there was a Christian kerygma; i.e., a kerygma proclaiming Jesus Christ — specifically Jesus Christ the Crucified and Risen One — to be God's eschatological act of salvation."[32]

However, this kerygmatic view faces two criticisms. First, this identification of the Bible with the kerygmatic statements seems to reduce the plurality of the biblical content to a single theme, Christology. As a result, in relation to the interpretation of the Old Testament, this kerygmatic approach has a tendency to degrade the Old Testament, seeing it merely as foreshadowing or prefiguring the New Testament, rather than as the First Testament of the Christian community of faith that is equally revelatory of God's divine activity in individual and communal lives.[33] Second, as Paul Tillich indicates, it is apt to overlook the theological task of responding to the particular situation of the contemporary context by overemphasizing the kerygma as "the unchangeable truth of the message over against the changing demands of the situation."[34]

Contrary to kerygmatic theologians' rigid and absolute understanding of the canonical quality of the Bible, Sanders claims that the Bible is "not a box of ancient jewels forever precious and valuable" but contains "a *paradigm* of the struggle of our ancestors in the faith against several forms of polytheism from the Bronze Age to the Roman Empire."[35] As Thomas Kuhn writes, paradigms are "accepted examples of actual scientific practice ... which ... provide models from which spring particular coherent traditions of scientific research."[36] In Christian theology, *paradigm* means a valid and essential structure or a constitutive theological pattern penetrating the complex aspects of the biblical content. It is used as an interpretive framework for a biblical text in relation to the contemporary context. Through the theological paradigm penetrating the Bible, the preacher sees, reads, and interprets a biblical text from his or her own congregational context. Here, it is important to note that the paradigm is not absolute. When an increasing number of problems that cannot be solved by the paradigm occur, that paradigm should be rejected and a new one accepted.[37] Therefore, any one paradigm or perspective in Christian theology cannot be the absolute norm by which all texts and all situations of the congregation must be accounted for.

In relation to this changing character of a paradigm, it is worth noting the metaphorical quality of the text. Metaphor was traditionally regarded as an "ornament of discourse," a decorative word or phrase. Its function was understood to have an emotional appeal rather than to influence the cognitive meaning of the discourse. However, Paul Ricoeur disagrees with this substitution theory. According to him, metaphor is more than a figure of style. It contains *"semantic innovation"* because as its unit is the sentence, metaphor includes "a decorative or referential dimension, i.e., the power of *redefining reality*."[38] Metaphor as a creative and imaginative poetic language re-presents our reality from a certain perspective and extends our cognition about reality beyond our present understanding. Whenever we open ourselves to the imaginative power of metaphor, it produces new meaning in relation to our particular experiences and enacts itself anew in our lives.

On the basis of this concept of metaphor, Sallie McFague claims that the Bible is a "poetic classic." It is authoritative because it has this metaphorical quality. She says that

> If we know God by the indirection of the Bible, then the Bible "is and is not" the word of God. The Bible is a metaphor of the word or ways of God, but as metaphor it is a relative, open-ended, secular, tensive judgment. It is ... the premier metaphor, the classic model, of God's ways for Christians, but as a metaphor it cannot be absolute, "divinely inspired," or final.[39]

The Bible as a metaphor is poetic in the sense that a biblical text is rich and diverse, open to many interpretations. And it is also a classic in the sense that it "lives beyond its own time as it meets and accommodates itself to the experiences and interpretations of diverse peoples." The Bible as metaphor is authoritative and valuable because it is "'timeless' in that it speaks a universal language through its own particularity, not because it says one thing, but because it can say many things."[40]

This metaphorical view of the Bible has had tremendous impact on contemporary homiletical theories. It particularly became the foundation for the development of narrative preaching in contemporary homiletics. David Buttrick in his *Homiletic* states the significance of metaphor in relation to preaching:

> What is preaching? Christian preaching tells a story and names a name. If narrative consciousness confers identity, then preaching transforms identity, converts in the truest sense of the word, by rewriting our stories into a God-with-us story — beginning, Presence, and end. But, in view of the great disclosure of Gratuitous Love, by metaphor, preaching renames the human world as a space for new humanity related to God. What preaching may do is to build in consciousness a new "faith-world" in which we may live and love![41]

While the metaphorical view enhances the interpretive quality of the Bible to the center of its authoritative elements, it has a weak side, too. As Elisabeth Schüssler Fiorenza criticizes, the metaphorical view presupposes the Bible to be a classic that includes ahistorical and atemporal characteristics and functions for all times to reflect unchangeable ontological patterns. However, it must be seen as moving from Scripture to classic, and not the other way around. Yet,

> Krister Stendal has argued that it is because of their authority as Scripture that the Scriptures have become classics and not that they have authority because they are classics. The Bible has become the primary classic of Western culture not because of its outstanding literary quality but because of its standing as the Scriptures which record divine revelation.[42]

Keeping this in mind, Schüssler Fiorenza defines the Bible not as a classic but as a "historical prototype"[43] or "the constitution of an ongoing community understood not as a set of laws, but as a set of interpretive practices that provide basic paradigms of Christian identity."[44] Her position stands for the canonical character of the Bible. However, she warns that the canonical approach without "critical evaluation"[45] is dangerous. It tends to authorize the male-dominant governing power of the church as the criterion for the authority of the Bible. Furthermore, it legitimizes the male-centered traditional interpretation of biblical texts as a justification for the ideology, which ignores the demands of the oppressed.[46] The authority of the Bible cannot be identified with the authorizing endorsement of the church. Rather, it depends on its interpretive capability as an "enabling resource" in relation to the contemporary experiences of oppressed women. It is authoritative not as a source but as "a resource of women's struggle for liberation."[47]

This theological review of understanding the authority of the Bible provides two insights for Asian American hermeneutics. First, it reveals that a paradigmatic and metaphorical view of the Bible that is concerned with developing a creative and transforming meaning of the biblical text corresponds to the functional understanding of the Asian scriptures as the vehicle for leading the spiritual life of the community. The view appeals to Asian American preaching in the sense that its goal is to guide the spiritual direction of the congregation through the biblical text. In spiritual preaching, the Bible is not limited by a rigid boundary in the literal and plain sense but is free to create a new meaning for the text metaphorically in relation to the particular experience of the congregation.

Second, Schüssler Fiorenza's radical view of the Bible as a resource for human experience challenges preachers to take seriously the context for preaching. The Bible is normative as long as it relates dialectically to the context of preaching based on an analysis of the congregation's situation. In this sense, the Asian American hermeneutic has an ongoing critical dialogue with contemporary experience and provides power to transform and liberate the congregation. Therefore, the preacher's "critical consciousness,"[48] which is the lens through which the text and the context are observed and penetrated, is an important element for biblical interpretation.

The Method of Interpretation

The Christian church traditionally used a two-step procedure for biblical interpretation, first turning to the ancient text (*explicatio*) and then to the congregational situation (*applicatio*). In this process, the text was understood to have two senses, literal and spiritual. In the early church, Origen of Alexandria insisted that biblical exegesis should aim to have a spiritual sense of the text beyond its literal sense because God through the divine Spirit was the author of Scripture and preferred allegorical interpretation to the literal or historical.[49] Augustine continued to stress the significance of the spiritual sense by stating in *On Christian Doctrine* that Scripture is composed of either things or signs. Things are learned by signs that signify something, and signs are either literal or figurative. For him, the literal or historical sense aids in revealing the figurative or spiritual meaning of biblical texts.[50] The standard medieval theory of biblical exegesis expanded this twofold literal-spiritual (or figurative) notion to a fourfold one by subdividing the spiritual sense into the three specific modes of allegory, tropology, and anagogy. Here, the historical or literal sense was considered to be the foundation of these multiple spiritual senses.[51]

However, the Reformers, influenced by Renaissance humanism, rejected the medieval preoccupation with the spiritual senses and emphasized study of the literal or historical meaning of the text based on grammatical and linguistic analyses. Martin Luther, although he was used to the medieval fourfold senses, accused the Roman church of exploiting the Bible in order to support the pope's power by means of allegorical interpretation and tried to understand the literal and tropological senses of the text.[52]

Since the development of historical-critical methods, biblical interpretation has tended to read behind the text. However, this approach broadened the gap between text and context and could not help the preacher bridge the distance between what it meant and what it means. It was not an easy task to bridge historical discontinuities between the text and the congregational context. In this situation, Barth emphasizes the significance of the "analogy of faith" as a means of grasping meaning from the text and proposes a threefold process of interpretation — *explicatio, meditatio,* and *applicatio.* According to him, the preacher first observes and investigates the text in its own historical context and explains what it meant. Such historical-critical methods as form criticism, redaction criticism, and word studies are the tools for discovering the original meaning of the text. Next, the preacher reflects on the text from a certain theological perspective. The text is meditated upon subjectively in relation to the particular experience of the preacher and the congregation. The last stage is the act of appropriation through which the preacher applies the already complete exposition of the text in the contemporary context of the listeners in order to determine what it means. Here, the medium of connecting the text and the contemporary context is the analogy of faith, which means that the relation between the content of the divine speaking and of the human hearing is analogically established by faith in God's self-revelation grounded in christological events.[53]

Although Barth's threefold approach seems to reinforce the simple two-step procedure, this method has several problems if we apply it to Asian American preaching. First of all, the process from explication through reflection to application presupposes that the value-free explanation of the text should be advanced before application. However, this polarity between explanation and application is practically impossible because, as Hans-Georg Gadamer indicates, every reader has a "prejudice" or "historically affected consciousness" when she or he encounters the text.[54] Thus, from the beginning of the interpretive process, explication and application are not separate but overlap, so that biblical interpretation for preaching cannot separate but must integrate them. Next, although Barth stresses the exegesis of the text by means of historical-critical methods, he does not address how to exegete the context. However, Asian American preaching regards the exegesis of the congregation as seriously as that of the text. The preacher as interpreter is not an independent agent but a representative of the interpretive community of faith and is required to know his or her own particular context for preaching. Furthermore, Barth's analogy of faith based on neo-orthodox theology seems to restrict the direction of understanding the meaning of the text from above (God's self-revelation) to below (human experience). This unilateral direction also leads biblical interpretation to a one-sided approach, from text to context. However, Asian American preaching treats both God's revelation and human experience with equal importance believing that the meaning of the text is created through mutual conversation between them rather than by a unilateral approach. The particular sociocultural experience of the Asian American congregation is an equally important source of connecting the text analogically for a new meaning of the text.

As an alternative to the traditional process from explication to application, Ricoeur's metaphorical process stands out. Ricoeur proposes a new paradigm based on his literary approach to biblical narratives. He maintains that interpretation should not follow a linear order from explication to application but should be dialectical, circulating "from understanding to explaining and then ... from explanation to comprehension."[55] Here, understanding means "a naive grasping of the meaning of the text as a whole" based on the interpreter's guess without the help of any scientific study of the text. While this stage is regarded as "primitive naivete," comprehension means "a sophisticated mode of understanding" validated by explanatory procedures through literary criticism and structural analysis. Ricoeur calls this stage a "second naivete" in and through biblical criticism.[56] In the process from explanation to comprehension, the richness of our contemporary experience is not ignored or reduced to an objective understanding of the text. Instead, the text is open-ended and redefines our identity and reality from our particular situation and experience.

This dialectical paradigm is also represented in Fred Craddock's proposal of biblical interpretation for preaching. In three chapters of *Preaching*, Craddock deals with interpretation concerning the listeners, the text, and between text and listener. Since the task of the preacher as interpreter is to create a particular meaning from the text for particular listeners in a particular situation, it is equally important for the listeners and the text to be exegeted and to have connections with each other through a certain interpretive process. Craddock's method of biblical interpretation can be summarized in three stages. After selecting a text, the preacher reads the text without any other resources or study aids. This is the stage of "primitive naivete" in Ricoeur's term. That is, it is "the time to listen, think, feel, imagine, and ask" with an open mind and heart in order to draw inspiration from the text. The preacher next keeps a distance from the text and investigates it with the assistance of biblical criticism. At this stage, dictionaries, atlases, and commentaries are helpful. The preacher refers to Greek and Hebrew texts or different translations in order to establish the text, determines the parameters of the text by placing it in the larger context, and views the text in its historical, literary, and theological contexts. Last, the preacher goes back to the text as pastor with an interest in his or her own particular congregation. The preacher derives meaning from the text by identifying its characters at a certain level with the listeners. This is the stage of the "second naivete," as Ricoeur says, in which the focus (what the text is saying) and function (what the text is doing) of the sermon can be applied to a particular congregation.[57]

Considering that Asian American preaching aims to create new meaning from the text based on the particular congregational experience, Craddock's method is attractive. It goes beyond both a precritical naive understanding of the text and a critical analysis of the text in order to gain new meaning for the listeners. However, before determining the method of biblical interpretation for Asian American preaching, it is important to consider the following two perspectives that help reinforce the metaphorical process.

One is represented by the critical insights of feminist and liberation theologians. According to Schüssler Fiorenza, since the historical background of the Bible reveals oppressive patriarchal sociopolitical structures and destructive androcentric ideologies, the preacher should read behind the text with a "critical consciousness."[58] In relation to this, she proposes a fourfold process of interpretation: a hermeneutics of suspicion, a hermeneutics of remembrance, a hermeneutics of proclamation, and a hermeneutics of liberative vision and imagination. The first is to detect and analyze androcentric presuppositions and patriarchal interests within both the biblical text and its traditional interpretation. The second is to reconstruct biblical history as the "history of women and men." The third is to inspect how much canonical texts contributed to the struggle for liberation. And the last is to retell the biblical stories from a liberating perspective and amplify the emancipatory voices suppressed in biblical texts.[59] According to Schüssler Fiorenza, biblical interpretation has liberating power only when the text is read with critical consciousness and constructed anew from the liberative theological perspective. This liberation theological perspective challenges preachers to read the text critically.

The other perspective is from Asian hermeneutics, in which meditation is taken seriously. Asian hermeneutics helps us realize the significant role of meditation and provides insights for turning biblical interpretation into a meditative process. Although the word *meditation* is not popular in Protestant hermeneutics, it is interesting to find its significant role in the practice of an ancient Christian meditative reading known as *lectio divina*, or divine reading. Audrey Sorrento defines this as a process through which the reader enters into the mystery of Christ, that is, a living contact with him, through reading the text slowly, prayerfully, and frequently.[60] The process of *lectio divina* follows four steps. In *lectio* (reading), you read a text slowly and with full attention until you are familiar with it. In *meditatio* (meditation) you engage in an intuitive way of thinking and knowing, using the imagination. Experience the text personally and deepen an interpersonal relationship with God. In *oratio* (prayer) you converse with God concerning your relationship with God and derive implications for your spiritual life by means of the intuitive faculties. In *contemplatio* (contemplation), following the guidance of the Holy Spirit in prayer, you empty yourself and experience the grace that God has given to you as a gift.[61]

Noteworthy is the similarity between Zen meditation and the practice of *lectio divina*. Thelma Hall sees common aspects between the process of divine reading and the instruction of meditation in Zen Buddhism as follows:

Lectio Divina	**Zen Meditation**
We read (*Lectio*)	Sitting still,
under the eye of God (*Meditatio*)	doing nothing,
until the heart is touched (*Oratio*)	Spring comes,
and leaps to flame. (*Contemplatio*)	and the grass grows by itself.[62]

Lectio divina was practiced throughout the Middle Ages among ordinary believers and monastic monks and nuns in order to nurture their spiritual life. However, by the end of the sixteenth century, it became an extraordinary practice restricted to an elite few in the Roman Catholic church and now is practiced by monks and nuns of the Benedictine-Cistercian tradition.[63] As a result, unfortunately, Protestant churches as a whole seem to have lost its significance and value as a formative instrument for the growth of Christian spirituality. Stanley Hauerwas regrets the contemporary tendency of North American Christians, saying that "North American Christians are trained to believe that they are capable of reading the Bible without spiritual and moral transformation. They read the Bible not as Christians, not as a people set apart, but as democratic citizens who think their 'common sense' is sufficient for 'understanding' the Scripture."[64]

In this context, the Asian American homiletics reasserts the significance of *lectio divina* in terms of its meditative process. It is applicable to developing a concrete method of spiritual reading. The difference between Asian meditation and *lectio divina* is that the former practices meditation in order for the practitioner to realize his or her own true self in the state of emptiness while the latter reveals truthful salvation by means of meditating on a specific text in the presence of the Holy Spirit. However, neither can be used directly as a method of Asian American hermeneutics because their approaches are too individualistic to interact with the contemporary experience of the congregation. Asian American hermeneutics is not only for the preacher per se but also for the sake of the congregation. The preacher as interpreter is sent to the text as the representative of the congregation in order to gain spiritual guidelines for the community of faith through active dialogue between the text and the congregational context. For this purpose, it is necessary for the Asian American homiletic to develop a particular method of spiritual hermeneutics and to discipline the preacher with that method.

Spiritual Hermeneutics

Spiritual hermeneutics emerges from the critical and comparative dialogue between Asian and Western hermeneutics. This is not an absolute idea or system but a model to help the preacher understand the Bible in a relevant way in the particular context for Asian American preaching and practice biblical interpretation effectively for creating meaning from the text in order to shape and nurture the congregation's eschatological spirituality. Spiritual hermeneutics understands the Bible as the manual of spirituality and develops the process of interpretation as an art of meditation.

The Bible as the Manual of Spirituality

The Bible is the norm of Asian American preaching in the sense that it is a collection of experience bearing witness to the presence and power of God. The Bible describes as the historical record the experience of God in particular times and places in various literary forms — narrative, poetry, proverbs, letters, apocalypses, and so on. However, this historicity does not reduce the Bible to being simply a book about the past. Rather, the biblical witnesses transcend their temporal particularity and relate as metaphor to our contemporary experience. Their metaphorical quality is open to the creation of new meaning beyond their historical characters and makes the biblical text for preaching become the vehicle for carrying the listeners to the strange new world of the kingdom of God.

Thus, the preacher reads the Bible neither as a value-neutral, scientific object that stimulates only intellectual curiosity nor as timeless rules and precepts that regulate and instruct the listeners' moral behavior. Rather, the Bible is the preacher's intimate partner in guiding the community of faith along its spiritual journey. The Bible is the source of creating a new vision for the future of the community of faith. The preacher whose task is to guide the congregation along the right track of their spiritual journey experiences the presence and power of the Spirit from the text and at the same time calls forth the experience of the congregation in order for them to listen to the will of God. Therefore, the Bible functions as the manual of spirituality of the congregation by mediating the relationship between them and the living God. It is authoritative because it is a primary source to shape a vision for the community and sustain the spirituality of the congregation.

Interpretation as the Art of Meditation

The method of biblical interpretation is as important as a mariner's compass. Just as the mariner's compass gives right directions on a voyage, so the method of biblical interpretation helps the preacher be able to discern, evaluate, and integrate the spiritual direction of the congregation from a given text. It is a dynamic process waiting for the inspiration of the Holy Spirit beyond human limitation, involving a penetration of the deep structure of the text through meditation.

The following is a proposed method of biblical interpretation for preaching based on the practice of meditation in the scheme of the metaphorical process. This is not an absolute method or system but a model to help the preacher read the text in the presence of God

and create a meaning for a spiritual direction of the community
of faith. The whole process of seven stages depends on guidance
from the Holy Spirit, and the stages are not linear but work as a
spiral.

Prayerful preparation. Biblical interpretation for Asian American
preaching is possible only when the Holy Spirit is present at the
time of interpretation. A new meaning for the guidance of the congregation's spirituality is created not merely by reasoning but also
by the experience of the intimate relationship between the preacher
and the divine Spirit. Thus, it begins with prayer through which the
preacher prepares to hear the text with a faithful heart. Prayer is the
medium to relate the interpreter to a deep knowledge and experience
of God. Through prayer, the preacher invokes the Holy Spirit and
asks for help for the whole process of interpretation. Prayer cleans
and opens the preacher's soul to listen for the Word of God and fills
it with divine grace and inspiration. In this manner, the process of
interpretation depends on the divine guidance of the Spirit from the
beginning.

Text selection. In *The Witness of Preaching* Thomas G. Long introduces four ways of selecting the text for preaching: (1) *lectio continua*,
in which a certain book of the Bible is read in sequence until the
whole book is used as text; (2) a lectionary, which is a list of biblical passages selected on the basis of the Christian church calendar
and scheduled according to christological events; (3) a local church
lectionary, which combines a lectionary with the congregational calendar of events and denominational program of special days; and
(4) a preacher's choice of text, depending on the preacher's pastoral
sensibility concerning the pressing needs of the congregation on a
week-to-week basis rather than following a systematic plan.[65]

The most important point concerning text selection is that no matter how the preacher selects the text, one must empty oneself of any
preunderstanding or prejudice about the text. The meaning of the text
is open-ended, and the Holy Spirit leads the preacher to recognize a
new meaning for the sake of shaping and nurturing the spirituality of
the congregation.

When selecting a text, it is necessary to determine logical places
for the text to begin and end, considering such factors as connectors

between paragraphs, shifts in style, mood, location, and activity before and after the given verses. The selected text needs to be either translated from the original language or compared with a variety of modern translations in order to arrive at the most accurate translation and to make smooth reading.

Attentive reading. After selecting the text, the preacher reads the text from the heart, without any aid of commentaries or articles written about the text. There are several principles for this reading. First, read the whole text slowly, aloud, and repeatedly in faith with active imagination until the whole text is memorized and engraved in the preacher's mind and heart. Do not concentrate too much on single words or sentences within the text. Instead, read comprehensively, concentrating on the whole text. Such meditative reading opens the preacher to reflect on meaning under the guidance of the divine Spirit. Second, do not hurry to gain something from the text; rather remain empty and wait on the Word of God until the Holy Spirit gives inspiration. Last, write down words or draw symbols and pictures inspired from particular insights, feelings, questions, or resolutions that you derive from the reading. Composing a song from them or moving to the rhythmic words of the text can also help stretch your intuitive and imaginative insights.

Critical understanding. Not all insights attained through attentive reading are useful for making a sermon. At this stage, the preacher reads the text critically in order to discern them with the help of biblical dictionaries, commentaries, and other exegetical resources. These works are not the primary tools for interpreting the text but are secondary resources for the preparation of preaching. However, knowledge gained from them relating to grammatical-philological questions about sentences and meaning of the words in the text, particular sociocultural conditions of the text, its literary form and deep structure, the author's intention, the canonical characteristics, and so forth helps the preacher clarify and deepen homiletical ideas acquired through attentive reading.

Sensitive listening. The preacher listens to the context with pastoral sensibility in order to discern the presence and work of God the Spirit in the daily lives of the congregation. At this stage, the preacher's sensitivity to the world in every detail is one of the most

effective keys to discern the work of the Holy Spirit in human lives. As Barbara Brown Taylor points out, it is "not a natural gift but an acquired skill."[66] The preacher's pastoral sensibility, based on imagination and intuitive faculties, plays an important role in grasping the deeper meaning of life and "the holiness hidden just beneath the everyday surface of things."[67] The preacher's personal life, ministerial experiences, and the indirect experience of living empathetically with diverse humanity can all help him or her increase that pastoral sensibility. Moreover, some information and knowledge from fields such as sociology, psychology, economics, politics, ecology, anthropology, biology, and history assist the preacher in identifying particular congregational issues and provide useful resources for theological reflection. In addition, as Craddock suggests, reading newspapers and interviewing community leaders like chiefs of police and school superintendents can help the preacher understand the congregation in the larger community where it resides.

Dynamic interaction. The two worlds of the text and the context are not separate but are interrelated from the beginning of the interpretive process. While the preacher investigates the text, the context already influences the preacher's consciousness and vice versa. The preacher sees, hears, touches, and smells the biblical characters, personalizes them imaginatively in relation to the contemporary listeners' experience, and senses the reactions of a variety of people. Through this dynamic interaction or "to-and-fro movement" between the world of the text and that of the context, the preacher narrows the gap between them; by viewing the text through many different eyes, the preacher may gain intuitive insight into new meaning for a sermon. This is a moment of enlightenment, a "movement through darkness to light."[68] Here, rewriting or paraphrasing the text helps clarify both the "center of gravity" of the text and the focus of a sermon.[69]

Theological reflection. The focus of the sermon gained through dynamic interaction between the text and the context is now reflected upon deeply from the Christian eschatological perspective. That is, the preacher deepens the meaning of the text, centering on what the text is going to say, and develops that focus to the function of the sermon, that is, what the text is going to do in a sermon in relation to the formation and nurture of the spirituality of the congregation.

At this stage, the preacher looks at the present reality from the perspective of the eschatological hope promised in the Bible and creates a new vision for the community of faith by experiencing a strange new world of the text. Likewise, the Christian eschatological perspective functions as a lens through which the preacher discerns a theological direction of interpretation.

However, it is worth noting that the influence is not always from theology to biblical interpretation but is often the reverse. In other words, although the Christian eschatological perspective presents a coherent picture of the revelation of God in biblical texts, it cannot force all biblical texts onto a grid because not everything in the Bible can be made to fit perfectly with this single theological view. Rather, the diversity of biblical passages reserves open-ended dialogue for the construction and progressive development of Christian theology and homiletical orientation. They are interdependent and reciprocal, influencing each other for the development of a contextually relevant theological perspective of preaching.

Conclusion

The proposal of spiritual hermeneutics for Asian American preaching suggests new insights into understanding the authority of the Bible and developing an interpretive method for preaching. The Bible is authoritative for Asian American preaching because it functions as the manual for guiding the spiritual life of the congregation. Its meaning is created through the seven stages of the meditative process.

Biblical interpretation for preaching is the disciplinary process of listening for the Word of God through the interplay of the biblical text and the particular experience of the congregation by the intercession of the Holy Spirit. It is a spiritual discipline that requires an active and responsible reading with the preacher's capacity for passion and an ardent love for the life of the congregation. Its ultimate goal is to lead the entire congregation to encounter the presence and work of God the Spirit in their daily lives as well as in the Bible and to encourage them to live as living parables of the kingdom of God.

Notes

1. See Rodney L. Taylor, *The Religious Dimensions of Confucianism* (New York: State University of New York Press, 1990), 23–24, 25, 28, 33, for the information in this paragraph.

2. The quotes are from Wing-tsit Chan, "Chu Hsi's Completion of Neo-Confucianism," in *Études Song-Sung Studies: In Memoriam Étienne Balazs*, ed. François Aubin, series 2, no. 1 (1973): 85, quoted in ibid., 33, 35, 34.

3. Xiaosui Xiao, "From the Hierarchical Ren to Egalitarianism: A Case of Cross-Cultural Rhetorical Mediation," *Quarterly Journal of Speech* 82 (1996): 43–44.

4. Ibid., 41–42. Contrary to Karl Barth's "analogy of faith," the "analogical projection" corresponds to Emil Brunner's "analogy of being."

5. Taylor, 80.

6. Wing-tsit Chan, trans., *Reflections on Things at Hand: The Neo-Confucian Anthology Compiled by Chu Hsi and Lu Tsu-Ch'ien* (New York: Columbia University Press, 1967), 121.

7. Ibid., 37.

8. Douglas A. Fox, *The Heart of Buddhist Wisdom: A Translation of the Heart Sutra with Historical Introduction and Commentary* (Lewiston, N.Y.: Edwin Mellen Press, 1985), 2.

9. Ibid., 47.

10. Miriam Levering, "Scripture and Its Reception: A Buddhist Case," in *Rethinking Scripture: Essays from a Comparative Perspective*, ed. Miriam Levering (New York: State University of New York Press, 1989), 63, 65, 64. The quotes are on pages 63 and 65.

11. Ibid., 61.

12. Ibid., 63.

13. Robert E. Buswell, "Ch'an Hermeneutics: A Korean View," in *Buddhist Hermeneutics*, ed. Donald S. Lopez Jr. (Honolulu: University of Hawaii Press, 1988), 246–47.

14. Edward Conze, trans., *The Perfection of Wisdom in Eight Thousand Lines and Its Verse Summary* (Bolinas, Calif.: Four Seasons Foundation, 1973), 266–27, quoted from Levering, 62.

15. Ibid., 70.

16. Ibid., 72.

17. A word used as an object of meditation is called *koan* in Japanese and *hwadu* in Korean. See chapter 5 for further explanation.

18. Daisetz Teitaro Suzuki, *The Field of Zen: Contributions to The Middle Way, the Journal of the Buddhist Society*, ed. Christmas Humphreys (London: The Buddhist Society, 1969), 25. The concept and definition of intuition

and the distinction between intuition and imagination are further explained in chapter 4.

19. Ibid., 21.

20. Christmas Humphreys, *Studies in the Middle Way: Being Thoughts on Buddhism Applied* (London: George Allen & Unwin, 1959), 82.

21. See Elisabeth Schüssler Fiorenza, *Bread Not Stone: The Challenge of Feminist Biblical Interpretation* (Boston: Beacon, 1984), 25–28; David Kelsey, *The Uses of Scripture in Recent Theology* (Philadelphia: Fortress, 1975), 18–37.

22. Schüssler Fiorenza, 25.

23. Ibid., 29, 30.

24. Later, Brevard Childs's *Biblical Theology of the Old and New Testaments* (Minneapolis: Fortress, 1992) and other biblical theologians' works emphasized the significance of the canonical character of the Bible and contributed to the development of canonical criticism in biblical theology.

25. Karl Barth, *Church Dogmatics*, trans. G. W. Bromiley (Edinburgh: T. & T Clark, 1975), I/1, 102.

26. Ibid., 106.

27. Kelsey, 105–6.

28. Ibid., 93.

29. Barth, I/1, 107.

30. Ibid., 107.

31. Ibid., 108.

32. Rudolf Bultmann, *Theology of the New Testament*, trans. Kendrick Grobel (New York: Charles Scribner's Sons, 1951–1955), 3.

33. Ronald J. Allen and John Holbert, *Holy Root, Holy Branches: Christian Preaching from the Old Testament* (Nashville: Abingdon, 1995), 31–33.

34. Paul Tillich, *Systematic Theology*, 3 volumes (Chicago: University of Chicago Press, 1951), 1:4–5.

35. James Sanders, *From Sacred Story to Sacred Text* (Philadelphia: Fortress, 1987), 5.

36. Thomas Kuhn, *The Structure of Scientific Revolutions* (Chicago: University of Chicago Press, 1970), 10, quoted from Garrett Green, *Imagining God: Theology and the Religious Imagination* (San Francisco: Harper & Row, 1989), 46.

37. Ibid., 47.

38. Paul Ricoeur, "Biblical Hermeneutics," *Semeia 4: Paul Ricoeur on Biblical Hermeneutics*, ed. John Dominic Crossan (Missoula, Mont.: Scholars Press, 1975), 75.

39. Sallie McFague, *Metaphorical Theology: Models of God in Religious Language* (Philadelphia: Fortress, 1982), 54.

40. Ibid., 59.

41. David Buttrick, *Homiletic: Moves and Structures* (Philadelphia: Fortress, 1987), 16–17.

42. Quoted from Elisabeth Schüssler Fiorenza, "The Crisis of Scriptural Authority," *Interpretation* 44 (1990): 353–68.

43. Schüssler Fiorenza, *Bread Not Stone*, 10.

44. Elisabeth Schüssler Fiorenza, *But She Said* (Boston: Beacon, 1992), 143.

45. Schüssler Fiorenza, *Bread Not Stone*, 135.

46. Schüssler Fiorenza, *But She Said*, 143.

47. Ibid., xvii, 14.

48. Ibid., 133.

49. *Interpreter's Dictionary of the Bible* (Nashville: Abingdon Press, 1962), 2:719.

50. Augustine, *On Christian Doctrine* 1.2; 2.15.

51. Karlfried Froehlich, "Always to Keep the Literal Sense in Holy Scripture Means to Kill One's Soul: The State of Biblical Hermeneutics at the Beginning of the Fifteenth Century," in *Literary Uses of Typology* (Princeton, N.J.: Princeton University Press, 1977), 23.

52. Eric W. Gritsch, "Luther's Humor as a Tool for Interpreting Scripture," in *Biblical Hermeneutics in Historical Perspective: Studies in Honor of Karlfried Froehlich on His Sixtieth Birthday*, ed. Mark S. Burrows and Paul Rorem (Grand Rapids, Mich.: Eerdmans, 1991), 196.

53. Barth, I/2, 722–40.

54. Hans-Georg Gadamer, *Truth and Method*, trans. Joel Weinsheimer and Donald G. Marshall (New York: Crossroad), 360.

55. Paul Ricoeur, *Interpretation Theory: Discourse and the Surplus of Meaning* (Fort Worth, Tex.: The Texas Christian University Press, 1976), 74.

56. Paul Ricoeur, *The Symbolism of Evil* (Boston: Beacon, 1969), 351.

57. Fred Craddock, *Preaching* (Nashville: Abingdon, 1987), 101–24.

58. Schüssler Fiorenza, *But She Said*, 52–53.

59. Ibid., 53–55.

60. Audrey Sorrento, "Meditation and the Bible: Expecting to Be Addressed by God," in *Scripture: The Word Beyond the Word* (New York: The Women's Division, General Board of Global Ministries, The United Methodist Church, 1985), 29.

61. John Westerhoff, *Spiritual Life: The Foundation for Preaching and Teaching* (Louisville: Westminster/John Knox, 1994), 72–74; cf. Thelma Hall, R.C., *Too Deep for Words: Rediscovering Lectio Divina* (New York: Paulist, 1988), 36–45.

62. Hall, 44, 47.

63. Ibid., 1.

64. Stanley Hauerwas, *Unleashing the Scripture: Freeing the Bible from Captivity to America* (Nashville: Abingdon, 1993), 15.

65. Thomas G. Long, *The Witness of Preaching* (Louisville: Westminster/John Knox, 1989), 62–64.

66. Barbara Brown Taylor, "Preaching the Body," in *Listening to the Word: Studies in Honor of Fred B. Craddock*, ed. Gail R. O'Day and Thomas G. Long (Nashville: Abingdon, 1993), 217.

67. Ibid., 218.

68. Hall, 55.

69. Long, 69. Long defines the "center of gravity" as "a main thought around which all other thoughts are organized."

Chapter Four

The Design of a Sermon

The sermonic form is an essential part of preaching. It serves preaching not only as the vehicle of the content but also as a major factor in creating the meaning of a sermon. As Thomas G. Long states, "A sermon's form, although often largely unperceived by the hearers, provides shape and energy to the sermon and thus becomes itself a vital force in how a sermon makes meaning."[1] Although there is no ideal or standard form for a sermon in Christian communities, as H. Grady Davis points out, each sermon may have its own particular form that is "inseparable from the content."[2]

Contemporary homileticians have developed a variety of creative ideas for designing a form that appeals to listeners. They agree that the sermonic form should be listener oriented rather than speaker oriented and that its primary concern should be how to approach effectively the ways the listeners can experience the sermon. David Buttrick says "we are children of a particular time and place, of a cultural epoch," so that our general way of communicating must be based on a common consciousness, culturally shaped by common language, attitudes, worldview, and ethos.[3] Thus, designing the sermonic form is a creative work based on the preacher's sensitivity and knowledge of communication theory. It requires of the preacher discipline and practice.

In order to develop some implications for designing the form for spiritual preaching to Asian American congregations, we must examine some distinctively Asian ways of communicating. If the sermonic form relates to the listeners' communication style, the preacher can more easily guide the congregation along a spiritual journey with an eschatological vision for the new community. An analysis of Asian ways of communicating not only will reveal their distinctive characteristics but also will identify grounds in common with contemporary Western homiletical theories. Insights gained from this analysis do not yield a single standard form of spiritual preaching, but they will help to develop some basic principles and general modes that can be applied variously and effectively.

Asian Ways of Communicating

China, Korea, and Japan have their own particular languages and verbal and nonverbal expressions influenced by geographical, historical, and cultural distinctiveness. They also share a high degree of similarity in their communication due to common philosophical and religious foundations. As organized religious systems, Buddhism and Confucianism have had an impact for thousands of years on the formation of Asian verbal and nonverbal communication as well as their values of life and ethos. Not only religious scholars, monks, and nuns but also laity have been shaped by Buddhist and Confucian teachings and religious practices. Both groups have observed religious ceremonies, festivals, and rituals.

The common characteristics of their communication can be summarized in four aspects: holistic knowing, the pursuit of consensus, the dialogue of silence, and indirect communication. Knowing these four components makes it possible to approach an understanding of the general fundamentals of Asian communication.

Holistic Knowing

While Western communication is rationalistic and focuses on intellectual understanding, the Asian way is holistic. It is based on the epistemological views of Confucianism and Buddhism. Confucianism maintains that the highest learning comes from a balance between intellectual study and intuitive meditation. It approaches humanity through human nature, including reason and feeling, and aims at the cultivation of the mind. The cultivation of humanity or self-realization is fulfilled when a fundamental unity or oneness between self and the universe is felt.[4] In Buddhist epistemology, intuition is regarded as the most significant cognitive faculty. Enlightenment can be experienced only by intuitive knowing. However, intuition in the Buddhist sense is not a separate human cognitive faculty contrasted to intellect and emotion. Rather, it is an integrating principle in which reason and emotion function together for the self-knowledge of the whole and the grasp of ultimate truth.[5]

Both religions' epistemological approaches to the realization of truth have encouraged Asian communication to be holistic rather than simply intellectual or emotional. They have come to develop a view that human nature is an integrated whole of intellect, emotion, and intuition. Asians believe that not only reason but also feelings are essential parts of human nature and function to affect the decision making and the actions of individuals and groups. Based on this understanding, Asians seek heart-to-heart, more than mind-to-mind, communication. Heart-to-heart communication is impossible with only the cold logic of reason. Rather, as Dean C. Barnlund, who is an expert in intercultural communication, correctly observes, it is based "on listening rather than speaking, on intuition rather than explanation, on synthesis over analysis."[6]

This view is reflected in both private and public communications. The experience of a young Jesuit missionary working in Japan exemplifies this. At first he had great difficulty in evangelism because his Western training, based on logical syllogism, clashed with Japanese communication style. Later he developed "affective communication" by realizing how the Japanese respected intuitive feelings and emotions in communications. He modified his logical syllogistic style with a lengthy talk around the point, with aesthetic and "soulful" words and expressions until the listeners *felt* how wonderful it was to be a Catholic. Through this communication method, he was able to accomplish his mission.[7]

This holistic characteristic in communication is well known in Asian marketing and advertising strategies. Because the Asian mental process moves holistically toward its objective in a sort of spiral, advertising does not move directly to reach the point it is trying to achieve. Rather, it brings up multiple visions by associating the objective with side effects. For example, posters and pamphlets often include not only a main photo and message but also, as background, poetic expressions and attractive scenery that appeal to the customer emotionally and intuitively.[8]

The Pursuit of Consensus

East Asian culture, influenced by Confucian and Buddhist spirituality, respects harmonious relations. Harmony and unity are more valued than difference and conflict. In this accommodation-oriented culture, the goal of communication is to seek agreement or consensus rather than disagreement or division. As a way of arriving at consensus, the speaker appeals to the heart of the audience. That is, rather than stressing points through a manipulative or coercive manner, which may clash with those of others, Asian persuasion seeks the audience's voluntary consensus with the speaker by guiding them to feel as the speaker feels, to see from the same perspective, and finally to be awakened intuitively as the speaker was.

This consensus-oriented communication must be carefully organized to be "cautious, tentative, complimentary toward the others, incomplete and seeking others to make the position complete."[9] In order to communicate in this way, stories and anecdotes are often used as effective forms. As an example, John Condon and Fathi Yousef illustrate the different styles between feminist writings in Japan and those in the United States. While American feminists stress "action: what's wrong, what must be done, and how to do it now," Japanese writers tell a story describing "the plight of women in Japan and then, sadly, just stop."[10] Through this seemingly incomplete style, the speaker seeks a voluntary consensus with the audience by letting them draw a conclusion for themselves. In this consensus-oriented style of communication, one must first create an "aesthetic and soulful" mood that brings forth a one-mind and one-heart condition between the speaker and the audience. This results from an honest, heartfelt approach to the audience by balancing their reason and emotion.

Likewise, Asian communication style seeks to lead the audience to participate actively in the speech act. The speaker does not give the audience direct advice or instruction for decision making or any action but guides them to a spot where they can discover something for themselves. It is the audience's job to connect speech to their own experience and come to a point of understanding through their own imagination and intuitive feelings. If the speaker provides the audience with a detail-oriented explanation or stresses his or her own point, the listeners may feel that the speaker is invading their area in the course of the speech.

The Dialogue of Silence

While Western culture generally tends to regard silence as a "communicative failure or evidence of a deteriorating relationship,"[11] Asian culture highly values its function in communication. Silence has long been an important form of communication in Buddhism. Silence does not mean an absence of meaning but a moment through which thoughts and feelings occur from emptiness. Meditation in silence is a way to reach the true mind and to experience enlightenment; it is the intuitive spark of the ultimate truth. This occurs when the meditator disconnects his or her thinking and feeling from memory and present experience because enlightenment is an experience of something new, of something different from anything of this world. This silent reflection was also adopted by Confucian scholars and practiced as a learning process.

In contemporary Asian communication, silence is regarded as an effective communicative form. It does not mean an embarrassing moment that occurs by a sudden break in the flow of words, but a comfortable tranquility that occurs when the speaker and the hearer identify so fully that they need no words to confirm their rapport.[12] A Japanese romantic scene illustrates the significant role of silence in communication:

> A young couple may sit together for hours and exchange no more than a half-dozen words while communicating as much and as well as their more verbal counterparts in other societies. Should the young man observe to his fiancée, "How beautiful is the moon," he will have communicated a proposal of marriage at least as clearly as his French counterpart would through many more words all related to the romantic prospects ahead.[13]

Silence in Asian communication has been practiced in "the space-oriented mode" of communication. The space between words and sentences allows the listeners or readers to pause, wait, imagine, and experience before moving on to the next image.[14] More precisely speaking, a writer or a speaker leaves space, pausing for some time between sentences or words, because verbalized images alone are incomplete for creative communication. Here, space or timing does not simply designate a meaningless void or state of naught but rather connotes a "reservoir of meanings" that provides the listeners or the readers with a reflective moment. It is a sort of aesthetic experience in communication shared by Asians. Muneo J. Yoshikawa illustrates a classical Japanese poem in order to show how space or silence between lines invites the reader to the creation of meaning.

> Old pond (ma)...
> Frog jumped in (ma)...
> The sound of water (ma)...[15]

Silence is a moment of active listening, reflecting things deeply, and grasping meanings intuitively. It is a time for memory and imagination, a time for creating meaning and decision making. In this sense, it is an active dialogue.

Indirect Communication

Traditional Western speech patterns are generally very direct. The speaker comes to the point directly and clearly by stating his or her own conclusion or generalized idea at the beginning of the speech and then proceeds to clarify or support that abstract or general statement with details.[16] By contrast, the Asian communication pattern is indirect. It begins with various particular experiences and ends with a unified, generalized point.

This indirectness is illustrated by Robert Kaplan's experimental study. Kaplan, who had analyzed the English compositions of Korean native speakers in his class, reported that while native English writers used a direct and straight movement like a vertical arrow from the opening sentence to the last sentence, Korean writers used an indirect approach. Their composition structure was "a widening gyre" turning and turning in a circle toward an inner point rather than a straight line. The circle or gyre turned around the subject to show it from a variety of tangential views until it reached the last sentence of the writing.[17] This indirect approach is also shown in Japanese and Korean grammar. For example, while English has a predicate verb right after the subject noun or pronoun, Korean and Japanese place the verb at the end of the sentence. The hearer does not know the speaker's intention or the whole meaning of the sentence unless he or she listens to the last word. Indirect communication is embedded in Asian speech habits, too. More frequently than Westerners, Asians use "apologetic and evasive statements like: 'It seems to be . . .'; 'It appears like . . .'; 'I dare say that . . .'; 'It may be (quite safely) said that . . .'; 'I am afraid that I may be wrong if I say that . . .'; and 'I agree with him but. . . .'"[18]

Moreover, such indirectness suggests the usual way of life in Asian social relationships and behavior. As an example, an American banker who had worked in Japan for several years reported that one of his frustrating and difficult experiences in dealing with Japanese business people was their indirect speech style. He, who was used to the American way of "coming to the point quickly," was uncomfortable with the Asian style of communication that talked around and around the focal point until finally arriving.[19]

Indirect communication is the predominant technique cultivated in Buddhism as a means of instructing the student to experience enlightenment. In the Buddha's own and later Buddhist masters' teaching methods, there are many stories and anecdotes that seem to be obscure and unrelated to the central point. Particularly in Zen Buddhism, a type of cryptic riddle (a *koan* in Japanese or *hwadu* in Korean) has served to guide the students to reach enlightenment by self-examination and self-reflection. This is a typical example of indirect communication between a Buddhist master and his disciple:

> A monk said to Joshu, "I have just entered this monastery. Please teach me."
> "Have you eaten your rice porridge?" asked Joshu.
> "Yes, I have," replied the monk.
> "Then you had better wash your bowl," said Joshu.
> With this the monk gained insight.[20]

This conversation may be ambiguous and off the point from the Western perspective, which anticipates a direct answer. However, as is the case with Jesus' parables in the Gospels, the master challenges the disciple to think about hidden meaning and to find its central point for himself by using his imagination.

Homiletical Implications

The Asian ways of communicating that we have examined suggest some homiletical implications for the development of the sermonic form of spiritual preaching. Interestingly, in some ways there exist common understandings between Asian communication theory and contemporary homiletics. The characteristics of Asian communication will be explored further by engaging themselves in dialogue with contemporary homiletical theories in an attempt to develop some homiletical implications for the design of the sermonic form for spiritual preaching.

Intuition as the Divine Communicational Channel

Western epistemology divides human consciousness into intellect, emotion, and intuition and regards intellect or reason as the most important cognitive faculty. This reason-oriented tendency is also found in the sermonic form of traditional European American preaching. The propositional point-making sermon has long been used as a means of giving the congregation a clear intellectual understanding of the content. However, the limitations of this model and benefits of the holistic approach to preaching have become major issue in homiletical circles. Henry Mitchell rightly points out that Western homiletical theories have paid little attention to the significant role of the intuitive and emotive sectors while overemphasizing the dimension of human rationality. He further says:

> Modern researchers are saying that [Christian faith] resides in the intuitive region, that great, right-brain storehouse, whose content has not been entered into the human data bank by rational criteria and processes. One must add that faith also resides in the emotions. If fear

is an emotion, then so is its opposite, trust. In other words, if one's
faith has no emotive dimension and involvement, it is cold and without
depth.[21]

Thus, reason functions only to help orderly understanding based
on a logical sequence of words and flow of images. Christian faith is
not born "*of* rational argument," nor does it proceed from a flow of
logical persuasion, but it exists in balance with intuition and emotion.
Therefore, preaching should appeal to the whole person, not only the
intellect but also the emotional and intuitive faculties.

Mitchell defines intuition as insight gained from cultural influence and individual experience, which is unconsciously stored in one's
personality. Intuition is communicational channel through which the
Holy Spirit encounters the individual. Through intuition, people can
enter the "spiritual-theological dynamics of an encounter with the
Godhead" and take part in the spiritual experience.[22] He understands
emotion to be passion or "deep feelings." Although it is often de-
graded because of its negative aspects of "fear, lust, hate, prejudice,
and paranoid distrust," emotion also has positive characteristics of
faith, hope, love, and joy.

Regarding these "godly emotions" as the source of nurturing the
Christian faith, Mitchell maintains that the highest goal of preaching is to help the congregation experience these feelings.[23] From the
perspective of the African American preaching tradition, he identifies preaching with "emotional rejoicing" or a time of celebration
in which the congregation participates in emotional and spiritual
ecstasy, enhancing their feelings with "sound and spontaneous emotional expressions." In order to fulfill this goal, Mitchell suggests that
the form of a sermon should proceed not as a "sequence-of-ideas"
but as a "flow-in-consciousness"[24] toward an emotional climax at the
conclusion of the sermon. This "ecstatic reinforcement" will cause
"great rejoicing and praise"[25] so that the congregation will experience
the Holy Spirit as present within their lives and working for them.
Mitchell's holistic approach is biased toward an emphasis on emotion. He understands the holistic approach to lead the congregation
to experience the climactic point of emotional celebration. Human intellect and intuition assist in moving toward this emotional climax in
preaching. This understanding reveals that Mitchell presupposes that

the three faculties of human consciousness work in the process of perception according to a certain linear order and that emotion is the last and the highest stage. As such, achieving the wholeness of human consciousness means reaching the final destination of emotion.

However, Mitchell's view of the emotion-centered linear order of the holistic approach is challenged by the Asian view. In Asian communication, intuition is the integrating center of human consciousness in which holistic knowing occurs, not by a sequential movement from one faculty to another but by experiencing sudden recognition. This holistic, integrative moment is an experience of oneness or unity of human consciousness. In this condition, human consciousness is not separated into compartments or stages. Rather, all the faculties work together as one as the individual experiences a timely, generative, comprehensive, and clear awakening moment of truth. Clearly, in Asian communication, intuition is not simply one aspect of human consciousness that assists in achieving an emotional climax or intellectual understanding but is a contributor to a condition of unity in which all perceptive faculties generate a spontaneous grasp of truth.

Although Western homiletical theories do not take intuition seriously, its nature and function as the epistemological basis have been prominent in the Western religious and philosophical studies. As Henri Bergson points out, intuition is not in opposition to intelligence, as Romanticism understands it to be, but is holistic and relational.[26] Consistent with the Asian view, it is associated with the whole person, joining itself to physical as well as mental experiences. Intuition gathers together "disparate images, impressions, sensations and ideas" and grasps "the overall sense of a person" to form a holistic perception.[27] What is distinctive about this intuitive knowing is its immediate character. It is by an "intuitive leap" that disparate cognitive elements are brought together to a single common place.[28] Intuitive knowing depends neither on analytic knowledge resulting simply from scientific research and logical proof nor on knowledge acquired by experience. Rather, a truth is known holistically and directly.

In relation to intuition, it is worth noting the concept of imagination that contemporary homiletics has brought to our attention. Although Aristotle limited imagination to the dimension of sensation

by defining it as "a sensory function which preserves sense data
and combines or associates them," contemporary theologians and
homileticians deal with imagination as one of the most important
factors in bringing the listener into a new experience of truth. They
understand it in general as a God-given human ability that enables
us to understand divine revelation. Imagination is the bearer of truth
that has the integrative power of human consciousness and uncon-
sciousness. However, it is not merely a natural gift or talent, says Paul
Wilson, but a skill or technique that is to be learned and improved
by training.[29] Barbara Brown Taylor considers imagination to be the
epistemological ground of preaching. She explains that

> imagination is the meeting place of God and human kind, the cham-
> ber between heaven and earth where the sacred and the commonplace
> mingle and flow in unexpected ways....It is the ability to make
> connections between two different frames of reference so that a
> spark is struck at the point where they intersect, illuminating a new
> possibility.[30]

Taylor's understanding is consistent with that of Garret Green.
Green, in *Imagining God*, surveys diverse definitions and functions of
imagination within the Western philosophical, religious, and scientific fields and defines the religious imagination as "the paradigmatic
(pattern-making and pattern-recognizing) faculty."[31] According to
him, imagination brings forth a certain level of perception just like the
experience of a paradigm shift, having a new and unanticipated con-
figuration, conversion, or transformation. It happens neither gradually
nor cumulatively but suddenly and discontinuously, so as to contribute
to a discovery of truth beyond human consciousness.

In relation to preaching, this function of imagination is of great
value. When a sermon form strikes the imagination of the listeners,
it enables them to connect the biblical story to their own particular experiences and transforms it into a saving story. Through this
imagination, then, it is possible for the preacher's human words to
have the transforming power of the Spirit. Thus, imagination used
by the Spirit has the power to generate, shape, and compose the
world of meaning in which we live and invent ways to reconstruct
that world from an eschatological perspective. At the same time, it

should be remembered this imagination is not always used in positive and productive ways. It can also be a venue for misunderstanding, illusion, and delusion. It may create fantastic worlds and bizarre categories with disastrous effects on personal integrity and communal unity unless it is nurtured in the context of the community of faith, the *koinonia*.

Considering the positive function of imagination, there are similarities and differences between imagination and intuition. Just like intuition, imagination functions to make the listeners experience an immediate and holistic change in their thoughts and actions. They may be associated with human intellect and feelings but may also transcend them. However, as Green indicates, imagination is based on a person's experience or prior knowledge while intuition emerges from emptiness or a void. More precisely speaking, imagination is understood in light of empiricism as an interpretive activity. It is an analogical perception, an ability "to see what something is like based on one's prior experience." In other words, imagination allows the interpretation of an object from a person's experience. Therefore, to imagine a new reality of the future is possible only through analogy of the past or present reality. For example, explains Green, the ability to see Wittgenstein's duck-rabbit metaphor either as a rabbit or a duck is based on the person's imagination, which depends "not only on the reception of sense data but also on prior experience and context. A person who has never seen a rabbit but is familiar with ducks will surely see a duck."[32]

By contrast, the intuitive awakening is a new experience that has never happened before. Just as intuition provides the Samaritan woman's awakening experience through her encounter with Jesus by the well or the awakening of the disciples who met Christ on the way to Emmaus, so it offers us the new experience of a strange new world in the Bible. It is beyond our conventional mode of thinking constructed on the basis of our prior knowledge or experience. In this sense, Victor Kal says that intuition is "a supra-human mind...the mind of God...which carries out a kind of abstraction in relation to the thoughts in the human mind."[33] It is a communicational channel between the human and the divine. It taps the spirit and participates in the formation and growth of spirituality.

Therefore, intuition or intuitive imagination is closely related to spiritual preaching because it embraces the wholeness of human consciousness. It provides spiritual preaching with epistemological access. If a sermon is designed to engage the congregation's intuition, it will directly affect their spirituality. Feeling so deeply touched and moved by the truthful message in the holistic intuitive process, the listeners will be guided to the self-realization of truth. Spiritual preaching that is a dynamic process actively waiting for the inspiration of the Holy Spirit requires a sermonic form that appeals to the human consciousness holistically. The holistic approach to intuitive knowing will enable spiritual preaching to be the communicational channel through which the congregation encounters the presence and power of the Holy Spirit. This notion raises a question: What kind of a sermonic form can appeal to the holistic consciousness of the congregation?

Consensus-Oriented Conversation

The goal of Asian communication as the pursuit of consensus is consistent with that of spiritual preaching in the sense that spiritual preaching aims at the unity and harmony of the congregation in an eschatological vision for the community. Accordingly, the sermonic form requires the congregation to participate in reaching a communal consensus as they move toward a spiritual direction.

As Asian communication implies, consensus can be achieved by a harmonious mood created by a full-blown conversation between the congregation and the preacher rather than by manipulating or coercing the listeners to the point that the preacher intends. Respect for the listeners' self-realization and self-decision is the basis of this conversation. In order for the listeners to be guided to participate voluntarily in the conversation, a carefully designed sermonic form is necessary. Moreover, the listeners are also expected to engage in the conversation with openness and empathy. The preacher and the listeners are interdependent, standing together as explorers seeking spiritual guidance for their community.

This view of preaching as a consensus-oriented conversation reminds us of Lucy Rose's proposal of "conversational preaching." In

Sharing the Word, Rose categorizes Western preaching into three types, traditional, kerygmatic, and transformational, and argues that all three types presuppose a gap between pulpit and pew. They share a regard for the preacher as an authority figure who is responsible for teaching, persuading, or transforming the congregation rather than as a conversation partner who shares the "tasks of discerning and proclaiming God's Word" with the congregation.[34] Instead, she proposes that the preacher and the congregation be "equal partners on a journey to understand and live out their faith commitments."[35] Thus, the preacher would not impose the results of his or her thinking but would invite the listeners to a process of thinking in order to help them interpret their experience for themselves.

Rose does not suggest any new idea or model as a sermonic form for conversational preaching but reaffirms the effectiveness of Fred Craddock's indicative approach and Eugene Lowry's narrative plot.[36] She reasons that the movement of inductive narrative form is controlled "not by objective logic, not even by the biblical story...but by the logic of the heart searching for wholeness."[37] This invites the congregation to reflect on their own experiences and faith journeys and to derive their own conclusions from the sermon.[38] Thus, she recommends that a combination of these two forms be used as a conversational preaching form.

Spiritual preaching is consistent with Rose's conversational preaching in the sense that neither aims to teach the preacher's own way or any particular way of life with authority but to guide the congregation to self-decision. However, the ultimate goals of their respective conversations are different. That is, the goal of Rose's conversational preaching is "nurturing a process" of thinking through conversation, while spiritual preaching's fundamental goal is not just to open the conversation but to create a mood of consensus among the congregation. Spiritual preaching does not merely initiate conversation about an issue on Christian faith or ethical life but guides the congregation to find a common ground for their faith journey and to help them decide on a common action to create a new community, the *koinonia*. At this point, the sermon form for spiritual preaching needs more than the narrative form.

Space-Oriented Communication

While Asians have regarded silence as an important factor in communication, Western homiletics has not paid attention to it. For example, traditional preaching form, which aims to transmit clearly the message that the preacher obtained while preparing for preaching, regards logical discourse and clear, direct verbal expressions as effective elements in the process of explanation, argument, application, and illustration. In this rationally logical form, there is no room for silence. Even contemporary homileticians who are concerned with the movement of the listeners' consciousness in order for them to experience the sermon have overlooked the significant role of silence in designing the form. This is curious in light of the fact that, outside of homiletics, Western communication theory has recognized the significant role of silence in communication. Thomas J. Bruneau, an expert in communication studies, indicates that decision making and problem resolution take place in moments of silence. Particularly, many possible meanings of a message can emerge through interactive silences, that is, "pausal interruptions in dialogue, conversation, discussion, debates, etc."[39]

The role of silence in preaching is worth exploring. Particularly when the sermonic form aims to bring forth intuitive awakening, silence is one of its major components. In Christian terminology, the intuitive awakening or enlightenment means the transformation of the human spirit by the Holy Spirit or their oneness. It occurs in the matrix of the holistic human consciousness — human feeling, willing, thinking, and discerning — through interaction between the human spirit and the divine spirit. It will happen in a meditative moment rather than in an abundant flow of verbal expression or logical reasoning. Although some preachers take seriously space or pausing in the delivery of a sermon as a means of effective communication, silence should be considered even when first designing the form. The sermonic form itself should be a space-oriented movement in order to approach the listeners' consciousness holistically.

Thus, just as hermeneutics of spiritual preaching involves the art of meditation through which the preacher listens to the text attentively, so the sermonic form also demands a meditative style that can give the listeners a moment to experience the Spirit. It will lead the congregation to complete the sermon by recognizing a spiritual guideline for themselves under the guidance of the Holy Spirit. Therefore, while emotional "ecstatic reinforcement" helps African American preaching arrive at an emotional climax or celebrative moment, the space-oriented flow of movement will assist spiritual preaching to be meditative preaching. Space-oriented meditative communication will enable the listeners to have time for self-decision and for reflecting on transforming actions for their life journey.

The Spiral Form as a Way of Indirect Communication

Remembering that spiritual preaching aims to guide the listeners to a holistic awakening to the truth in the communal context, indirect communication, which has been culturally embedded in Asians, seems to be an effective communication method. Although the indirect approach is inappropriate for objective research papers or science projects, it is valuable for helping listeners experience the moment of the self-realization of truth.

In fact, contemporary homiletics has emphasized the indirect approach as a powerful way of telling the Christian truth. Craddock stresses its validity and usefulness for preaching in three ways, quoting Søren Kierkegaard. First, indirect communication suits "the nature of the Christian religion" because God has revealed God's self indirectly in and through the human form, Jesus Christ. Christian truth is hardly communicated by direct communication. Second, the church must communicate its Christian message to the listeners in a way that is "inwardly appropriate" rather by a way that adds more information to the listeners' minds. Thus, indirect communication leads them to the realization of truth rather than to the accumulation of information. Third, the direct method cannot be the primary communication style for pastors because it often results in opposition, defensiveness, or disillusionment between the pastor and the congregation.[40]

In addition to these reasons, Craddock further urges the effectiveness of the indirect approach in preaching from the perspective of contemporary American thinking. He is convinced that the fundamental way Americans communicate is inductive.

> There are now at least two generations who have been educated in this way from kindergarten through college. Experience figures prominently in the process, not just at the point of receiving lessons and truths to be implemented, but in the process of arriving at those truths. Because the particulars of life provide the place of beginning, there is the necessity of a ground of shared experience.[41]

How, then, can preaching be indirectly communicated? Craddock insists on the inductive approach. If the traditional deductive sermon has a rigid structure beginning with a proposition or general truth and ending with a particular application or explanation, the inductive sermon is the reverse. It begins with the particular experiences of the congregation, so that the congregation arrives at the destination of the sermon together with the preacher through a reflective journey of their particular experiences.[42] As an example, story or narrative has this inductive movement and invites the listeners to be active, not passive, participants in the story. Likewise, in inductive preaching, the decision making is not done by the preacher but by the listeners for themselves. That is, they are invited to participate in the completion of the thought.[43]

While Craddock's notion of inductive movement provides a direction of the flow for spiritual preaching, Lowry offers a more concrete approach. He maintains that the indirect approach to the sermon does not mean including some stories or anecdotes as illustrations or examples but making the sermon itself a kind of story designed with a "narrative plot" and "sequencing strategy," much as playwrights, scriptwriters, and novelists do. In *The Homiletical Plot*, he proposes five stages of that plot: upsetting the equilibrium; analyzing the discrepancy; disclosing the clue to resolution; experiencing the gospel; and anticipating the consequences.[44] These stages are connected to each other as a sequence moving toward the denouement. In his later book, *The Sermon*, Lowry simplifies this narrative plot into four stages, which he explains like this: "its plot form, . . . begins with a felt *discrepancy* or conflict, and then makes its way through *complication* (things always get worse), makes a decisively sharp turn or *reversal*, and then moves finally toward *resolution* or closure."[45] As Lowry explains, the narrative plot or a sequence of movements follows "the logic of listening not just the consistency of conceptual categories."[46] The listeners are approached indirectly. They experience the sermon as their own story by relating the message to their own experience and arrive at their own conclusion.

Although both the inductive and narrative sermon forms seem to be readily used for indirect communication, the Asian communication theory introduces a spiral form as another way of indirect communication. This is a typical indirect approach turning around and around the subject until it reaches the central point. Although it is similar to the other two forms as an indirect approach, it is distinctive in the sense that the spiral form is a series of cyclical movements "winding around a center or pole and gradually...approaching it."[47] By contrast, the inductive form is a straight, linear movement toward the conclusion, and the narrative form moves to a point of "sudden shift" or reversal. As a sermonic form, the spiral form may seem at first glance to be unrelated to the subject matter of the sermon. But it is very clearly moving toward the central focus because each cycle illumines the focal point from a certain distance, gravitating to it. This spiral-form sermon is further explored in the following section by means of an exemplary sermon.

The Spiral-Form Sermon

A Buddhist sermon by Ronald Y. Nakasone represents a spiral form.[48] The outline of his funeral sermon moves in four round cycles like a spiral gravitating to the central theme. First, he addresses death at the existential level as one of the human karmic events in the course of a lifetime. With compassionate words, the preacher helps the listeners view their suffering as a universal human predicament that they cannot predict or escape. In the second round, death is viewed at a personal level, psychologically and emotionally. The preacher brings the mourners' deep feelings of isolation, grief, anguish, pain, and anger at the merciless world to the surface and helps them accept grief as reality. In the third round, death is viewed beyond sorrow in a community context as the mystery of life through which the listeners experience essential humanity. That is, all the community members realize the significance of the Buddhist doctrine of interdependence. The preacher reminds the listeners of this truth through a direct communication, saying that

> all beings are inextricably bound together in a community.... Humanity is one single body, one living Buddha body. What touches one part of this body touches all. Touch one strand and the entire web vibrates. Humanity shares a single destiny.... We all celebrate the birth of a child. Likewise we all mourn the passing of a child. We rejoice and grieve as one living body.[49]

In the last round, the preacher tells an anecdote of Sakyamuni Buddha and a young mother who had lost an infant child. While hearing the story, the listeners identify with the young mother and are encouraged to cultivate their own spiritual path. This last stage is followed by meditation.

As this sermon shows, this spiral movement has the following characteristics. First, it approaches the listeners holistically. As each cycle appeals to the listeners' reason and their feelings, each cycle has a potential for the listeners to experience a moment of enlightenment. The listeners may be deeply touched or moved at any cycle and arrive at the focal point through the last path of the cyclical journey. In this movement, the listeners understand the sermon in multiple ways around its subject matter based on their "diverse listening styles." As Long says, "Preachers may be passing out eggs, but hearers are making omelets, and a sermon preached to seventy-five people is actually transformed by them into seventy-five more-or-less-related sermons."[50]

Second, although the spiral form is overall an indirect approach, after the mood is fully developed, it also employs some direct explanations in order to help the listeners grasp the truth.[51] Through this combined method, the spiral form connects the three moments of understanding: "immediacy, reflection, and praxis," to borrow Buttrick's terms. That is, it causes "an immediate forming of understanding; a reflecting on understanding; and a looking at the world in a new way through understanding."[52] Buttrick places sermons in three categories based on these three types of understanding. The spiral form embraces all three in one sermon and guides the listeners to a holistic understanding of spiritual direction. This spiral form is an effective way to guide the congregation's spirituality because it may be used to invite the listeners to contribute to the event of the preaching with their own experiences and lead them to arrive with the preacher at the conclusion of the sermon.

Third, the spiral movement is designed not in any tightly formed way but in "a free-flowing, loosely connected way"[53] for the sake of the listeners who apply their own experience to the subject matter. It provides enough space for them to feel the guidance of the Holy Spirit for realizing a truth. In other words, it is a space-oriented movement. It takes timing seriously and allots proper space or pauses between moves in order to give the listeners meditative moments. This is especially important at the end of the sermon. At this moment, the preacher and the listeners seek and deepen the meaning of the sermon and reflect on their communal spiritual journey in light of the Christian eschatological perspective. It is time for self-decision and action toward an eschatological vision for the community. Likewise, the verbalized images alone are incomplete for spiritual preaching. The fully ripe mood of meditation at the conclusion of preaching ensures that the preaching is a spiritual experience and naturally leads to prayer after the sermon.

Last, in the spiral form, the story plays an important role in creating a consensus. In Asian communication, stories and anecdotes are usually used as the heart-to-heart communicational tools to bring forth unity and harmony among the audience. This is why Asian theologians are interested in story theology and stress its relevance as "the authentic medium of God's revelation."[54] However, considering that spiritual preaching should guide the congregation's spiritual journey with a new vision for the world, not all stories qualify for spiritual preaching, unless they reflect a part of the universal human experience. In other words, a story must interweave individual experience with the whole historical, sociocultural, and spiritual experience of the community, through which the listeners may be bound together as one and identify themselves as "we." Thus, the spiral form is a path of building up the sermon as "our" story.

Conclusion

Homiletical implications derived from a dialogue between characteristic Asian ways of communicating and Western homiletical theories
suggest that the sermonic form for spiritual preaching be indirectly
communicated in a spiral form. The characteristics of the spiral form
are indirect, holistic, conversational, and meditative. This form enables the listeners to experience the truth holistically through the
indirect movement of the spiral winding around a focal point. Each
cycle gravitates toward the subject matter of the sermon harmoniously in order to lead the congregation toward self-realization and
action from the eschatological perspective. Its space-oriented movement leads the congregation to a meditative moment through which
the Holy Spirit may guide the listeners along their communal journey
of Christian spirituality.

Notes

1. Thomas G. Long, *The Witness of Preaching* (Louisville: Westminster/
John Knox, 1989), 93.

2. H. Grady Davis, *Design for Preaching* (Philadelphia: Muhlenberg,
1958), 9.

3. David Buttrick, *Homiletic: Moves & Structures* (Philadelphia: Fortress,
1987), 296.

4. Young-chan Ro, *The Korean Neo-Confucianism of Yi Yulgok* (New York:
State University of New York Press, 1988), 45.

5. Daisetz Teitaro Suzuki, "Reason and Intuition in Buddhist Philosophy," in *The Japanese Mind: Essentials of Japanese Philosophy and Culture*, ed.
Charles A. Moore (Tokyo: Charles E. Tuttle Company, 1967), 66–69.

6. Dean C. Barnlund, *Communicative Styles of Japanese and Americans:
Images and Realities* (Belmont, Calif.: Wadsworth, 1989), 129.

7. Edward T. Hall, *The Hidden Dimension* (New York: Doubleday, 1990),
152.

8. David Rearwin, *The Asia: Business Book* (Yarmouth, Me.: Intercultural
Press, 1991), 69–71.

9. John C. Condon and Fathi Yousef, *An Introduction to Intercultural
Communication* (New York: Macmillan, 1987), 242–43.

10. Ibid., 242.

11. Barnlund, 143.

12. Ibid., 143.

13. Condon and Yousef, 19.

14. Muneo J. Yoshikawa, "Japanese and American Modes of Communication and Implications for Managerial and Organizational Behavior," a paper presented at the Second International Conference on Communication Theory from Eastern and Western Perspectives (July 1982): 53.

15. Ibid., 31. *Ma* means "space" or "betweenness."

16. Condon and Yousef, 240–41.

17. Robert B. Kaplan, "Cultural Thought Patterns in Intercultural Education," *Language Learning* 16, nos. 1 and 2 (1970): 6, 10.

18. June-Ock Yum, "Korean Philosophy and Communication," in *Communication Theory*, ed. D. Lawrence Kincaid (San Diego: Academic Press, 1987), 77.

19. Hall, 151.

20. This *koan* is from *The Gateless Gateway*, a collection of forty-eight *koans* compiled in the thirteenth century by the Chinese monk Mumon, quoted from *The Meditative Way: Readings in the Theory and Practice of Buddhist Meditation*, compiled by Rod Bucknell and Chris Kang (Richmond, Va.: Curzon, 1997), 66.

21. Henry H. Mitchell, *Celebration and Experience in Preaching* (Nashville: Abingdon, 1991), 19–20.

22. Ibid., 24–25.

23. Ibid., 27–28.

24. Ibid., 49.

25. Ibid., 63.

26. Henri Bergson, *The Creative Mind* (New York: Philosophical Library, 1946), 36.

27. Clarisse Croteau-Chonka, *Intuition: A Paradigm of the Wholeness Necessary for Holiness and Its Relationship to Christian Education* (Ph.D. diss., Princeton Theological Seminary, 1986), 155.

28. Ibid., 162–63.

29. Paul Scott Wilson, *Imagination of the Heart* (Nashville: Abingdon, 1988), 16.

30. Barbara Brown Taylor, "Preaching the Body," in *Listening to the Word: Studies in Honor of Fred B. Craddock*, ed. Gail R. O'Day and Thomas G. Long (Nashville: Abingdon, 1993), 213.

31. Garret Green, *Imagining God: Theology and the Religious Imagination* (San Francisco: Harper & Row, 1989), 94.

32. Ibid., 72.

33. Victor Kal, *Philosophia Antiqua: On Intuition and Discursive Reasoning in Aristotle* (New York: E. J. Brill, 1988), 14.

34. Lucy A. Rose, *Sharing the Word: Preaching in the Roundtable Church* (Louisville: Westminster/John Knox, 1997), 95.

35. Ibid., 89.

36. Craddock's inductive form and Lowry's narrative form sermons will be discussed later in this chapter in "The Spiral Form As a Way of Indirect Communication."

37. Lucy A. Rose, "The Parameters of Narrative Preaching," in *Journeys Toward Narrative Preaching*, ed. Wayne Bradley Robinson (New York: Pilgrim, 1990), 30.

38. Rose, *Sharing the Word*, 114.

39. Thomas J. Bruneau, "Communicative Silences: Forms and Functions," *The Journal of Communication* 23 (March 1993): 28–29.

40. Fred Craddock, *Overhearing the Gospel* (Nashville: Abingdon, 1978), 83–84.

41. Fred Craddock, *As One Without Authority* (Nashville: Abingdon, 1971), 58.

42. Ibid., 57, 61.

43. Ibid., 64.

44. Eugene L. Lowry, *The Homiletical Plot: The Sermon As Narrative Art Form* (Atlanta: John Knox, 1978).

45. Eugene L. Lowry, *The Sermon: Dancing the Edge of Mystery* (Nashville: Abingdon, 1997), 23.

46. Ibid., 59.

47. *Webster's New Collegiate Dictionary* (Springfield, Mass.: G. & C. Merriam Company, 1973).

48. Ronald Y. Nakasone, "Sermon Notes for a Forty-nine Day Memorial Service," in *Ethics of Enlightenment: Essays and Sermons in Search of a Buddhist Ethic* (Fremont, Calif.: Dharma Cloud Publishers, 1990), 85–89.

49. Ibid., 87.

50. Long, 131.

51. Refer to the third round of Nakasone's sermon.

52. Buttrick, 321.

53. Long, 132.

54. Nam-Dong Suh, "Theology as Story-Telling: A Counter-Theology," *CTC Bulletin* 5, no. 3 (December 1984): 7; cf. C. S. Song, *Tell Us Our Names: Story Theology from an Asian Perspective* (Maryknoll, N.Y.: Orbis, 1984).

Chapter Five

The Use of Language

In spiritual preaching, language is an important tool. Language makes it possible for preaching to invite the listeners to engage in thinking, perceiving, experiencing, and acting rather than merely recording a transmitted message. Through language, reality is re-presented, new meaning is created, and the power and presence of God are realized. And language functions in a broader way. That is, the existence of a common language basic to the cultural and spiritual life of the community of faith serves as a criterion for the identification of the congregation. Thus, spiritual preaching based on the religious and cultural experience of the Asian American community requires preachers to be sensitive in their use of language and to discipline themselves to use language adequately and effectively.

Most Asian American churches are bilingual because their immigration history is relatively short compared with those European American and African American communities. While Asian Americans use English in society, they use their native tongues at home and at church, often mixing the native tongues' words and idioms with English or vice versa. Asian American churches follow two patterns. Some hold two Sunday worship services, one in the native tongue and the other in English. Others hold one service with two languages. Considering that language is the form of expression and the "structure in which life is lived,"[1] this bilingual situation of Asian American congregations is one of the most typical examples of their lifestyle between two cultures, Asian and American. This implies the existence of a cultural and communicational gap between the native-language group and the English-speaking group in a church. It gives rise to the possibility that this language gap may cause conflict not only among the members but also between the preacher and the listeners.

129

This reality signals the preacher in a bilingual congregation to be more conscious of language use than is the preacher in a monolingual congregation. It challenges the preacher to develop rhetorical skills that can appeal to both groups. The native-language group and English-speaking group are different in thinking and perceiving depending on how acculturated they are in North American society. Still, there may be an effective rhetorical approach for them based on their common cultural ethos. Considering their cultural status of inbetweenness, the search for a model of homiletical language through cross-cultural dialogue is promising.

With this in mind, this chapter focuses on the question What kind of homiletical language is effective for spiritual preaching? The analysis of Asian rhetoric relating to the concept of language and its use in Buddhism and Confucianism helps rediscover cultural elements embedded in the Asian American community. Dialogue between Asian and Western rhetoric suggests some homiletical implications to develop the language of conversation for spiritual preaching.

Language in Asian Rhetoric

The three East Asian countries of China, Korea, and Japan share the characteristics of their languages. Korean and Japanese have been influenced by Chinese language and culture due to their geographical proximity to China. It is easy to find similarities among them in even the most superficial ways. As Jung Young Lee indicates, their languages are all nongendered. Since there is no different pronoun for male or female in these East Asian languages, they have less difficulty with gender issues at the divine level. In addition, singularity is often interchangeable with plurality so that "I" and "we" are mutually inclusive. For example, Koreans say "our house," "our mother," or "our God," meaning at the same time "my house," "my mother," and "my God."[2] Moreover, Confucian hierarchical order influenced these languages to develop plain, polite, and honorific levels of speech.[3] While English defines the speech level by address forms such as first name or title plus last name, East Asian languages represent different levels through pronouns, verbs, and nouns. Although the communist government in mainland China has destroyed this Confucian influence on Chinese spoken language under the banner of forming an egalitarian society, Korea and Japan still keep this hierarchical character.

At a deeper level, commonality among the East Asian languages is revealed by investigating the roots of their rhetorical traditions and the characteristics of their rhetorical perspective. It is useful for us to approach Asian rhetoric in general through Buddhist (especially Zen Buddhist) and Confucian rhetoric. There is a general but incorrect belief among many non-Asians that in Asian culture verbal language is treated skeptically "with the least confidence of all placed on the spoken word."[4] However, this prejudice, which is based on a superficial observation of Asian rhetoric, is dismantled after one examines Buddhist and Confucian rhetoric. Buddhist scriptures, Chinese classics, and other inherited written and oral materials of religious communication show that Asian rhetoric takes seriously the use of language and has developed particular rhetorical perspectives and techniques.

Buddhist Rhetoric

Buddhism seems to understand language to be generally inadequate to describe the truth. It tends to either underestimate it as "an avoidable and optional element" or disregard it as the "obstruction" to experiencing intuitive awakening,[5] because the intuitive sense of the mind happens by moving "behind" the words. Although the Buddhist concept of enlightenment is known as a direct and unmediated experience gained by meditation, language is still considered equally important as silent meditation. Language is a medium through which meditation and enlightenment are experienced.

The validity of the use of language in Buddhism is based on two stages, the negation of language and the negation of negation. Buddhist rhetoric first of all negates the use of conventional language. Although language exists as a means of human communication by which we try to express ourselves, it often restricts our experiences, thoughts, and feelings by limiting them to "our habits of verbalization and rationalization."[6] So, the dilemma of human communication is that reality cannot be apprehended or expressed fully in words. Without realizing this limitation of language, we are caught in the trap of language and easily become its slave.

However, when we are aware of this limitation, language can be our intimate friend. It can play a major role in mediating between everyday life and transcendence, making spiritual awakening possible. It functions like a raft or a finger:

> When we cross a river, we need a raft but when we have used it and reached the other side, we should discard it....When we point to the moon with a finger others are apt to take the finger for the moon. Yet without the finger the moon is not recognized, and when the moon is recognized the finger can be thrown away.[7]

Conventional language is not able to serve this mediating function because of its triteness and staleness. Instead, the language of enlightenment takes a new form, which is released from ordinary logic and conventional values. It is stretched to approach the inventive and creative in order to inspire a sudden awakening. As a vehicle for the practice of enlightenment, language seeks to "free its speakers and hearers, writers and readers, from the constraints of conventional modes of human comportment."[8] Dale Wright explains this practice of the negation of negation in Zen Buddhism:

> a Zen way with language is necessarily "unusual." Zen texts and the masters who are credited with having spoken them are famous for their improvisation along unconventional lines.... Zen discourse of this sort fulfills its function precisely as a transgression on everyday language and common sense. In the disorientation that results from it, the interlocutor or reader is himself [*sic*] thrown into question, sometimes by upsetting his [*sic*] normal position as the one who understands and acts on the world as subject. The "otherness" of Zen language is most powerful in the pressure that it places upon subjectivity. It introduces radical discontinuities into the subject's world and seeks some kind of significant disclosure as a result.[9]

This typical mode of language used by Buddhist rhetoric is called a *koan*. *Koans* are metaphorical narratives and poetic verses that have been created, amplified, and codified since ancient times. The *koan* includes anecdotes, poetry, legends, biographical details, and sayings of the great patriarchs, mostly in the conversational form between two masters or between master and disciple. Their mode of language follows neither propositional or syllogistic patterns nor conventional discursive styles but reflects wit and humor; their meaning is so paradoxical and mystical that it cannot be understood by intellectual analysis but "by heart" through spiritual discipline. Thus, Buddhist rhetoric "transcends the negations of rational language and dialectical logic."[10]

Koans are often misunderstood by Westerners to be cryptic riddles or puzzles whose trick is in their clever and obscure wording. However, this is not so. Rather, as Robert Aitken explains, *koans* are "the clearest possible expression of perennial facts which students grasp with focused meditation and guidance."[11] Their literary styles and metaphorical expressions challenge students to practice deep spiritual meditation and to gain profound wisdom. This *koan* offers a taste of its typical language:

> When Ch'an [Zen] Master Kuang-yung first went to visit Ch'an Master Yang-shan, the latter asked him, "What is the purpose of your visit?"
>
> Kuang-yung answered, "I came to pay my respects to the Master." Then Yang-shan inquired, "Have you seen the Master?"
>
> Kuang-yung replied, "Yes, I have."
>
> "Does the Master look like a donkey or a horse?"
>
> Kuang-yung answered, "It seems to me that the Master does not look like a Buddha either!"
>
> Yang-shan insisted, "If the Master does not look like a Buddha, then what does he look like?"
>
> Kuang-yung replied, "If he looked like something, then we would be no different from a donkey or a horse."
>
> Surprised, Yang-shan declared, "One should forget the difference between a Buddha and an average person and overcome all passions. Then One's true nature will shine. In twenty years, no one will be able to surpass you. Take care of yourself!"
>
> Later, Master Yang-shan told everyone, "Kuang-yung is a living Buddha."[12]

The *koan* has no final or single interpretation but is itself multivalent. One hundred *koans* give one hundred perspectives. But when they are enriched with insightful comments and poems, then they have ten thousand meanings, and there is no end to this process of enrichment.[13] The language of *koan* is simple, poetic, metaphorical, and conversational. In this sense, *koans* are like Jesus' parables. Both function to bring the listeners to the point where they open up for them a new dimension of experience and create a new meaning of life based on that experience. The *koan* is a medium of teaching and of meditational practice. It is an important tool along with meditation for the experience of sudden awakening. Therefore, in Buddhist rhetoric, language and meditation are reciprocal and interdependent as they move toward the goal of enlightenment.

Confucian Rhetoric

As Xing Lu points out, the Confucian classics themselves are a well-developed source of Asian rhetoric. Since most of these classics were written during a period of political chaos between 600 B.C. and 300 B.C. in order to seek social, political, and ethical reforms in society and to persuade readers to change their views and behavior, these writings reflect highly cultivated rhetorical skills sensitive to the power and impact of language.[14] According to Lu's analysis, Confucius was well aware of the impact of language on human perceptions and actions and himself was "a master of speech and language." His works, such as the Spring-Autumn Annual and the *Analects*, are full of "embellished, refined, and artistic use of language."[15]

The Confucian classics have influenced Asians to understand the nature and function of language realistically and practically. They have been a primary source for guiding ethical and moral life. The characteristics of Confucian rhetoric in relation to the use of language can be summarized in three respects. First, Confucian rhetoric understands language not as a mere means of communication but as a profound way of being human. As the ideal goal of Confucianism is to become a sage, the process of becoming a sage is related to the discipline of language because the individual's morality is reflected in his or her language use.[16]

Since the main function of communication according to Confucian philosophy is to initiate and develop social relationships, there is a strong emphasis on the proper use of language in communication. Good communication based on "the language of sincerity," which is "careful, truthful, spoken at the proper time, and given in a serious manner,"[17] participates in promoting social relationships. In contrast, "empty, flowery speech lacking in moral content would disturb the social order and lead people astray."[18] Condemning glib, clever, and superficial speech, Confucius asserts that "one who has accumulated moral power will certainly also possess eloquence; but he who has eloquence does not necessarily possess moral power."[19] Even in today's Asia, embellishment and flowery words in speech give the impression of being "glib, boastful, shallow, and untrustworthy." Instead, those who speak with "substance, wisdom, appropriateness, and humor" are highly appreciated and respected.[20]

Second, language in the Confucian classics is simple, crisp, and vivid as well as analogical and metaphorical. It is often "characterized by techniques of rhythm, antithesis, alliteration, and parallelism."[21] For example, we read in the *Analects* that

> He who does not understand the will of heaven
> cannot be regarded as a gentleman.
> He who does not know the rites
> cannot take his stand.
> He who does not understand words
> cannot understand people.[22]

The *Analects* is a collection of wise sayings much like Proverbs and Jesus' Sermon on the Mount. They are enlightening and easy to memorize. Thus,

> many of his [Confucius'] four-character phrases in the *Analects* have become popular Chinese sayings. The brevity, balance, and rhythm of classical Chinese language made it eminently well suited for the creation of proverbs, which not only helped with memorization, but also,...helped bridge the gap between the intellectual elites and common people in the world of Confucius.[23]

Moreover, analogy and metaphor are major techniques in Confucian rhetoric. Confucius believed that good analogies and metaphors helped reveal the principles of humanity. They were treated not simply as rhetorical devices or ornaments but as rhetorical methods of persuasion in order to give direction for sagehood. As an example, in order to advise his disciple who slept during the day, Confucius said

> Rotten wood cannot be carved,
> nor a wall of dried dung be trowelled.[24]

Third, the Confucian classics employ a dialogical pattern as a basic literary framework. In fact, the entire book of the *Analects* is written in the form of private conversations with questions and answers between master and disciples. In this mode of speech, Confucius used poetry and narrative with compact and concise expressions. He seemed to know that simple, poetic, and metaphorical language was more effective than discursive language for the purpose of responding to the social, cultural, and philosophical questions of his disciples. As an example, Confucius says in the *Analects* that

> Tzu-kung asked, What must a man be like in order that he may be called a true knight (of the Way)? The Master said, He who
>
>> In the furtherance of his own interests
>>   is held back by scruples,
>> Who as an envoy to far lands
>>   Does not disgrace his prince's commission
>
> may be called a true knight.[25]

It is also worth noting that among many literary forms poetry played a major role in Asian rhetoric not only in cultivating aesthetic pleasure but also in exchanging information. Oral poetry was also one of the most popular literary genres both in the Chinese classics and in the vernacular.[26] Poetry was used either as a single communicational form or as a part of narrative discourse. Poetry and narrative were often mixed in works of literature. Such a combined style, which was called the "lyric-narrative" form, was especially used to express a vision for the future world or "utopian yearnings"[27] similar to apocalyptic eschatological discourse in the Bible. When a fully articulated discursive language fails to communicate the imaginative properties of the vision, lyric as "a part of poetic consciousness" may express its intent.[28] But lyric alone cannot be an alternative to discursive language because its expression is limited to internal feelings and has difficulty describing the external. Here, the narrative framework may assist lyric in communicating external elements "through the minimum description of situation and narrative of actions."[29] Thus, in the lyric-narrative form, poetry and narrative are interdependent in accommodating the totality of the reader's cultural, social, ethical, and aesthetic experience.[30] The content is based on narrative reality while the language is poetic — indicative, descriptive, and metaphorical.[31]

Homiletical Implications

While an examination of Asian rhetoric reveals that it corresponds to contemporary Western homiletics in certain ways, the characteristics of Asian rhetoric discussed above present some rhetorical qualities that can be developed in relation to preaching. Particularly the three elements of Asian rhetoric — the negation of language, the use of poetic and metaphorical language, and the use of a private conversational pattern — suggest possibilities for engaging in a dynamic dialogue with Western rhetoric and its homiletical theories. A new perspective for the language of spiritual preaching and a way for its practice can emerge from this dialogue. This new understanding of the concept and use of language for preaching will contribute to complementing and deepening homiletical theories in general.

The Limitation of Language and God's Accommodation

The Buddhist perception of the limitation of language challenges the preacher to review the value of language. Without language, there exists no preaching. Through language the preacher and the congregation engage in thought and dialogue. Through language the community of faith shapes Christian belief and nurtures faith in Christ. However, language is not the perfect vehicle to transmit the mystery of Holiness, the mystery of God in Christ, and the mystery of the Holy Spirit into the life of the congregation.

David Buttrick in *Homiletic* rightly indicates that our ordinary language is too limited to express the mystery of God and says that "there may well be a world beyond the world shaped by language in which we live."[32] Our human language is restricted to regulated grammar, inexact vocabulary, and customary patterns. It is so limited to our particular historical, sociopolitical, and cultural context that it is unable to describe all human experience involving perception, feelings, imagination, and transcendental reality. The totality of our experience, knowledge, and thought are inevitably reduced when communicated through language.[33] Quoting Joseph Sittler and Robert Browne, Lucy Rose also argues convincingly that "all language, including the language of faith, is inevitably biased and limited, historically conditioned, and inseparable from the sins of each generation and each community of users."[34]

Acknowledging the limitations of language leads us to confess human imperfection when preaching the gospel and raises some homiletical questions: Is preaching a mistaken endeavor? Must we preachers be silent, remembering Wittgenstein's warning, "What can be said at all can be said clearly.... Whereof one cannot speak, thereon one must be silent"?[35] Or, is preaching still possible in human language in spite of its limitations? If so, in what sense?

Facing this language issue, spiritual preaching reevaluates the significance of the doctrine of God's accommodation and takes it into account for the theological foundation of preaching. The God about whom we preach is Spirit beyond our limited language. If our God-talk is possible, it is so only by the mercy of God who lowers God's self to our humanity. "In order to communicate effectively with human beings, God condescended, humbled, and accommodated [God's self] to human categories of thought and speech."[36] God's incarnation in Jesus of Nazareth is the climax of that accommodation. Moreover, the entire Bible is full of God's accommodated character. That is, the divine condescension to speak and act in the human form is revealed in the accommodated character of biblical language. God relates to us by using all varieties of human speech forms in order to mediate the distance between the divine and the human and to help us experience the mystery of the divine.[37]

Preaching is the ultimate form of God's accommodated communication. Human language, in spite of its imperfection, is adopted for preaching to accomplish God's perfect, divine function of bringing salvation for our benefit. Thus, preaching is neither solely divine nor solely human. Rather, it is a cooperative and interdependent act between the divine and the human. Without human language, the

Word cannot be heard. But, as John Calvin claims, "without the illumination of the Holy Spirit, the Word can do nothing." The Holy Spirit enables human speech to accomplish God's purposes by effectuating it beyond its limitations. So, "the Word becomes efficacious for our faith through the Holy Spirit."[38] Therefore, homiletical language is empowered by the intercession of the Holy Spirit, pointing to the realm of mystery, to the experience of God. Because God graciously condescends to use our limited language as a vehicle for communicating with us, we preachers can unashamedly preach the mystery of God in our limited language, convinced that "God can do something in, with, and through gospel-message speech."[39]

On the basis of this doctrine of God's accommodation, spiritual preaching has the right to use human language in order to help the listeners experience the mystery of God. Spiritual preaching negates the negation of language and employs human language actively as the primary tool for directing the spiritual journey of the congregation. At this point, spiritual preaching requires that preachers take homiletical language seriously and discipline their language for preaching. Here, the discipline of language does not simply mean learning "the language of Scripture and tradition"[40] but acquiring the means to express today's language and culture.

What kind of human language, then, is effective to reveal the mystery of God? Dialogue between Asian rhetoric and contemporary homiletical theories reveals that metaphorical and poetic language stretches ordinary human language beyond its conventional meaning toward the mystery of the divine.

The Use of Metaphorical Language and Eschatological Vision

Buddhist and Confucian rhetoric uses simple, metaphorical words to generate a sudden, intuitive awakening or a truthful thought about humanity. Poetic and analogical expressions both in *koans* and in the Confucian classics play a major role in helping listeners or readers gain a new perspective on life. Contemporary homiletics also pays attention to the significance of metaphorical and poetic language as a vehicle for carrying a truthful message.

Historically speaking, Protestant preaching rooted in the Calvinist tradition has preferred the plain, simple, and everyday language of ordinary people, the "emptying out of all that is ornamental, as exemplified in the work of Isaac Watts, who 'had to lay his poetic glories aside, and dress the profound message of the gospel in homespun verse and the language of the people.'"[41] However, contemporary homiletics as represented by Craddock, Buttrick, Lowry, Thomas Troeger, and others runs parallel with Asian rhetoric in mutual regard for metaphorical and poetic language. Both agree that ordinary language should be stretched to be metaphorical in order to express the transcendence and immanence of the divine. Buttrick maintains that

> preaching reaches for metaphorical language because God is a mysterious Presence-in-Absence. God is not an object in view. Therefore, preaching must resort to analogy, saying, "God is like..." The use of analogical language — metaphor, simile, image, and the like — is inevitable, and, obviously, desirable in preaching.... Moreover, because figurative language does draw on images of lived experience it is "incarnational" and, therefore, natural to a gospel of God-with-us.[42]

Whereas our everyday language is too conventional to speak of the mystery of God, the extended forms of metaphorical and analogical language broaden the experiential horizons of people and lead them to reach for the divine reality.

Just as Asian rhetoric uses poetic language, simple but intensive, subtle but precise, so the metaphorical dimension of the language in homiletics is heightened by poetic language. Robert Browne identifies a sermon with a poem in the sense that both depend on using words in a special way "in order to create a special effect upon those listeners and to light up the world for them."[43] Both preacher and poet use words to evoke images and create new meaning by carrying the richness of the metaphorical meaning. How, then, can the preacher be a poet? Browne instructs that

> You can never be a poet unless you are fascinated by words — their sound and shapes and meanings... the poet develops his [sic] poetic faculty through contemplation — that is to say, by looking steadily both at the world outside him [sic] and the things that happen inside him [sic] by using all his [sic] senses to feel the wonder, the sadness and the excitement of life, and by trying all the time, to grasp the pattern and help others to grasp it too.[44]

Poetic language can be characterized by its pictorial character. The preacher re-presents, rather than presents, his or her thoughts through imaginative pictorial language and causes the congregation to perceive those truthful thoughts. Poetic language creates a vivid and imaginative mood that is best suited to the intuitive awakening of the listener. It also has the quality of compactness. Compared with prosaic language, poetic language contains fewer words but makes a stronger appeal to the senses and emotions. Crisp and concise, rich and compact are the qualities of poetic language. A story told in poetic language is always more concise and compact than a story told in prosaic language. It is often heard rhythmically and appeals holistically, with power to evoke a feeling of empathy between speaker and listener and to invoke the mysterious experience of the divine beyond ordinary human experience.

In relation to poetic language, it should be noted that poetic language is not limited to the literary genre of poetry. It exists not only in poetry but also in other forms of communication. Both Asian classics and the Bible actively use poetic language in a variety of literary forms, including story, parable, anecdotes, and dialogue. As we have seen, most Buddhist *koans* consist of dialogue between two persons. On the surface, they seem to be an ordinary conversation. But their deeper language is metaphorical and poetic. Subtle and multivalent words in the dialogue break through ordinariness and challenge the interlocutor's conventional way of thinking and ultimately lead him or her to sudden awakening. Likewise, apocalyptic eschatological discourse in the Bible employs metaphorical and poetic language in order to unfold a vision of a new world. Because it is hard for the author to speak about that vision — a new heaven and a new earth — with direct communication, and because the author has critical insight into this world and wants to evoke a different vision of the world as fresh revelation, the author has to use poetic and metaphorical language. Thus, symbolic images such as resurrection and *parousia* can be understood only metaphorically and imaginatively within the particular context of the reader.

In this way, metaphorical and poetic language helps preaching awaken the listeners to perceive a truthful way along their spiritual journey. It opens a new world; it has "the protean power of its symbols to emit new meaning,"[45] stirring the listeners' hearts, minds, and souls to enlightenment and action. Spiritual preaching is concerned not with teaching a lesson or giving moral exhortation but with guiding the spiritual journey of the congregation. Therefore, its language should "violate the boundaries of ordinary secular language and transfigure it."[46] Through metaphorical and poetic language, spiritual preaching creates the expectation of a radically new reality in God's promised future. It participates in creating harmony and unity in the world, anticipating the fulfillment of God's promise.

Religious Discourse as Private Conversation

It is worth noting that Asian rhetoric considers a dialogical pattern to be the most effective mode of religious discourse. Both Buddhist texts and Confucian classics use dialogue between master and disciple or between masters as the basic communicational pattern. The private conversation pattern is helpful for revealing a truth to the reader or the hearer. The propensity for using the private conversational pattern in Buddhism and Confucianism implies that religious discourse is this private conversation rather than oratorical public speech. In relation to preaching, this reminds us that the term *sermon* is rooted in Latin *sermo*, whose original meaning is "private conversation."[47]

Classical Roman rhetoric also understands religious and philosophical discourse to be private conversation, *sermo*. In dealing with speaking and the voice in his *De Officiis* (On Duties), Cicero divided the *vis orationis* (power of oratory) into two parts: *contentio* (argument) and *sermo* (conversation). As Robert W. Cape Jr. translates it:

> *Contentio* should be ascribed to the debates in the courts, public assemblies, the senate, and *sermo* should be involved in social circles, in philosophical debates, and in meetings of friends. It should also follow after banquets. The rhetoricians have rules for *contentio*, none for *sermo*, though I do not know why they can't apply in this case too. Teachers are found when there are students desirous for learning, but there are none who desire to learn this [*sermo*], while all the rhetorician's crowds are packed. Yet the same rules of using words and phrases also apply to *sermo*.[48]

As Cape's study indicates, in ancient Rome *sermo* was a female style of speech. This mode of speech was not taught at school since it was regarded as an informal, women's way of communicating. However, it was very influential in Roman society because women educated their children at home, thereby affecting their sons' social speech skills. Although there exists no handbook on *sermo* per se, because rhetoric was taught only to men in Western society as a course of formal education, we can see a glimpse of the rhetoric for *sermo* in Cicero's *De Officiis*.

> The voice should be clear (*clara*) and pleasant (*suavis*) (1.133). Conversation (*sermo*) should be light (*lenis*), witty (*lepos*), and not obstinate (*minimeque pertinax*)....One must pay attention to the conversation to keep it on track, to make sure it is pleasant and that it has a reason for its beginning and a proper way in which to close (1.135). Finally, sermo ought to be free from extreme emotion and should not give rise to anger, covetousness, laziness, or idleness. "We ought to take the greatest care to show respect and have a special regard for those with whom we conduct our conversation" (1.136). In conversation one should never be harsh or angry, though it may be necessary to appear angry sometimes.[49]

It is interesting to realize that Cicero's instructions for *sermo* are consistent with those of Confucian rhetoric regarding the language of sincerity and its manner of politeness.

While the rhetoric for *sermo* had long been buried in the field of Western rhetoric and ignored by predominant male rhetoricians, late nineteenth- and early twentieth-century female rhetoricians rediscovered its significance. Jane Donawerth in "Textbooks for New Audiences" introduces three women who were professors of rhetoric — Gertrude Buck (1871–1922) at Vassar College, a women's school; Hallie Quinn Brown (1845–1949) at Wilberforce, a black coed college; and Mary Augusta Jordan (1855–1921) at Smith College, the largest women's institution in the United States.[50] They shared the feminine perspective on communication and emphasized the feminine style of speech as a general model for discourse.

Based on the experience of women students' communication, Buck presented rhetoric "not as dominance but as a means of equalizing speaker and hearer, writer and reader."[51] Brown and Jordan also revised their rhetorical theories to include a consideration of women's experience and their language. Both considered private conversation a rhetorical model and placed conversational language at the center of their rhetorical theories. They stood together on the premise that public and private discourse were not separate but lay on a "continuum from private to public."[52] So, in order to overcome the gap between speaker and audience in public speech, it was suggested that the speaker adopt the skills of private conversation. Donawerth evaluates Jordan's rhetoric of conversation as "far different from the prescriptive and psychologically manipulative eighteenth-century rhetorics most often taught in nineteenth-century male colleges." In her rhetoric, the audience was not to be "dominated, cajoled, or bullied."[53] Rather, her rhetorical goal was "social harmony and self-knowledge."[54]

This discussion of the rhetoric of private conversation reminds us that spiritual preaching as a form of religious discourse is neither a political campaign speech nor a courtroom testimony. It is neither a science project report nor a classroom lecture. It is, rather, private conversation with questions and analogies such as those used in personal dialogue between close friends or between mother and child or between teacher and student. Spiritual preaching is *sermo* between preacher and congregation, who have a common identity in faith and a common goal for the pursuit of truth.

The Language of Conversation

If spiritual preaching is private conversation, its language should be conversational. The language of conversation can be characterized in the following ways. The language of conversation is colloquial and casual. Remembering that homiletical language that is poetic and metaphorical best points to the mystery of God, it is necessary to connect metaphorical and poetic language to ordinary, everyday language. The combination of these two language modes in proper proportion allows preaching to be intimate, personal, and relational. If homiletical language is rigidly confined to set metaphorical and poetic expressions, preaching may run the risk of distancing itself from the listeners' daily lives. Instead, when metaphorical and poetic words are rediscovered in the congregation's everyday world, they can be woven into casual and colloquial language. Such homiletical language draws the listeners' attention and appeals to them naturally. It has power to create a new meaning, "dancing the edge of mystery, reaching into depth."[55]

Conversational language is successful only when it is based on the authenticity of the leader and the openness of the interlocutor. Both Asian rhetoric and Western homiletics rooted in Greco-Roman rhetoric take seriously the relationship between the speaker's authenticity and the impact of his or her own language on the listeners. Since Aristotle emphasized the ethos of the speaker as the most important factor in persuasion, the character and personality of the speaker have been regarded as one of the most influential elements in Western homiletics. Charles Campbell reinforces this view by maintaining that "preaching is not just an abstract language, but is embodied in the character of the preacher, the tone and inflections of speech, and the manner of delivery, just as a piece of jazz improvisation is inseparably related to the character and spirit of the musician."[56] The significance of the preacher's authenticity is also echoed in the perspective of Korean Neo-Confucian scholar Yi Yulgok. He claims that language is not a mere means of communication but "a profound way of being human."[57]

Furthermore, the preacher's religious and spiritual experience influences the choice of language and its creativity as much as does the preacher's personal character. Barbara Blaisdell puts it this way: "We [preachers] must be honest about our own doubts, questions, and experiences as we prepare to write. This part of preaching task is confessional. The final sermon need not be autobiographical, but it must reflect the real issues and struggles of a person of faith."[58] Rose also stresses the confessional character of language in relation to her proposal for conversational preaching. She extends the category of confessional language beyond personal to encompass a communal dimension, contending that "sermonic language is confessional, reflecting the accumulated and ongoing experiences of the people of God."[59] It should reflect the convictions of the community as well as the preacher's personal convictions because preaching is interpersonal communication in the language of "the *common shared vocabulary* of a congregation."[60] Preaching is a mode of conversation between congregation and preacher who belong to the same community of faith. Just as preaching arises within the community of faith, homiletical language is shaped by sharing the personal and communal experience of the members.

The language of conversation for spiritual preaching uses such diverse modes of speech as descriptive, indicative, imperative, and interrogative and uses them eclectically in order to fulfill the specific function of a single sermon. Descriptive language may help the preacher generate poetic imagery and intuitive inspiration and have the listeners experience the presence of God. Indicative statements may be useful both in declaring the promise of God in Jesus Christ and in making preaching to be the event of promising. It may also be used to exhort the congregation to participate in God's eschatological vision, thus carrying imperative force for the reciprocal responsibility of the community of faith, *koinonia*. The interrogative mode may have an imperative effect by challenging the listeners to struggle for a new world or may lend itself to a confessional style. With these various modes of speech, spiritual preaching employs a variety of literary genres such as poems, stories, confessional statements, a set of debates or explanations, or proverbs in its sermonic form as "a doorway of opening into a larger room of understanding and experience."[61]

How, then, can the preacher bring discipline to the language of conversation? Reflection on my own preaching experience suggests that the language of conversation is the language of a private letter. Writing a personal letter to a close friend, a former teacher, a parent, a child, or a spouse is a process of private conversation. Humor and wit, affectionate and empathetic feelings, poetic and metaphorical expressions are all involved in letter writing. A private letter may include stories, poems, memories, anecdotes, exhortations, or information in a dialogical form. It is a live dialogue, although it has a written form. It is heart-to-heart communication between the sender and the receiver.

At this point, it is understandable why the most prominent literary genre in the New Testament is the epistle. The communication style of the epistles is that of a private conversation based on the common identity between the sender and the receiver. By means of conversational language adorned with various literary styles, the letters bring the receivers to a sense of intimacy with the sender, making it possible for the sender to communicate the message of Jesus Christ effectively.

Likewise, the language of a private conversational letter is the language of the sermon. Writing a sermon for the congregation is like writing a letter to those who are in a close relationship with the preacher. The preacher and the congregation have a common identity as believers and are on the same spiritual journey together. The language of conversation — confessional and honest, simple and crisp, witty and humorous, poetic and metaphorical — can be developed by writing a private letter.

It is notable that Jordan stresses letter writing as a rhetorical discipline for the rhetoric of conversation by saying that letter writing requires

> skill in presentation, vividness of detail, choice of significant subject matter, evidence of delicate and precise knowledge of the reader's taste and character, and just so much revelation of the writer's self and interests as shall really serve the reader's. . . . In a letter, as in conversation, the other person should be left something of the topic to deal with. Letters should not be simply "unpublished works," but part of a pleasurable give and take, of suggestion, comment, interested question, and generous self-expression. The form might be after this sort: Something about me, something about you, something about the wide world.[62]

Jordan's view supports the intimate relationship between the language of conversation and the language of private letters. Therefore, if the preacher has the skill to write a moving letter, I am sure that preacher would employ the language of conversation effectively for spiritual preaching.

Conclusion

A cross-cultural approach to the rhetorical study of Asian and Western rhetoric helps to develop the language of spiritual preaching. The rhetorical insights gained from Buddhist and Confucian rhetoric, which can be summarized as the negation of language, the use of metaphorical and poetic language, and the use of dialogical form, engage in a dialogue with Western rhetoric and homiletical theories to develop a new idea for the language of conversation.

The language of conversation is grounded in the theological affirmation of God's accommodation and stretches ordinary language to express the mystery of God through metaphorical and poetic language. Like private conversation, its strength depends on its dialogical character. The language of conversation can be developed by private personal letter writing, whose characteristics are identified with those of the language of conversation.

When the preacher disciplines his or her words and uses them effectively for conversation about the gospel in Christ, the Holy Spirit renews our limited human language, and our words become the Word, the presence of God.

Notes

1. John C. Condon and Fathi Yousef, *An Introduction to Intercultural Communication* (New York: Macmillan, 1987), 196.

2. Jung Young Lee, *The Trinity in Asian Perspective* (Nashville: Abingdon, 1996), 78, 82, 65.

3. June-Ock Yum, "The Impact of Confucianism on Interpersonal Relationships and Communication Patterns in East Asia," in *Intercultural Communication: A Reader*, ed. Larry A. Samovar and Richard E. Porter (Belmont, Calif.: Wadsworth, 1994), 75–86.

4. D. Lawrence Kincaid, "Communication East and West: Points of Departure," in *Communication Theory*, ed. D. Lawrence Kincaid (San Diego: Academic Press, 1987), 336.

5. D. S. Wright, "Rethinking Transcendence: The Role of Language in Zen Experience," *Philosophy East and West* 42 (1992): 114.

6. Mark L. McPhail, *Zen in the Art of Rhetoric: An Inquiry into Coherence* (New York: State University of New York Press, 1996), 1.

7. Daisetz Teitaro Suzuki, *The Field of Zen: Contributions to the Middle Way, the Journal of the Buddhist Society*, ed. Christmas Humphreys (London: The Buddhist Society, 1969), 250.

8. Wright, 126.

9. Ibid., 128.

10. McPhail, 6.

11. Robert Aitken, trans., *The Gateless Barrier: The Wu-Men Kuan (Mumonkan)* (San Francisco: North Point Press, 1990), xiii.

12. Hsing Yun, *The Lion's Roar: Actualizing Buddhism in Daily Life and Building the Pure Land in Our Midst* (New York: Peter Lang, 1991), 2–3; for a poetic style of *koans*, see Haiku, Dodoitsu, and Waka, *A Zen Harvest*, comp. and trans. Soiku Shigematsu (San Francisco: North Point Press, 1988).

13. Robert Aitken, Foreword in *Book of Serenity*, trans. Thomas Cleary (Hudson, N.Y.: Lindisfarne Press, 1990), ix.

14. Xing Lu, *Rhetoric in Ancient China, Fifth to Third Century B.C.E.: A Comparison with Classical Greek Rhetoric* (Columbia: University of South Carolina Press, 1998).

15. Ibid., 166.

16. Arthur Waley, trans., *The Analects of Confucius*, book 1, 14 (New York: Vintage, 1989), 87.

17. *Yolgok Chônsô* (Seoul: Seongkyunkwan University, Taedong Munhwa Yonguwon Press, 1971), 1:330, quoted from Young-chan Ro, *The Korean Neo-Confucianism of Yi Yolgok* (New York: State of New York University Press, 1988), 106.

18. Lu, 163.

19. *The Analects of Confucius* (trans. Waley), book 14, 5, p. 180.

20. Lu, 31.

21. Ibid., 166.

22. *The Analects of Confucius* (trans. Waley), book 20, 3, p. 233.

23. Lu, 166.

24. *The Analects of Confucius* (trans. Waley), book 5, 9, p. 109.

25. Ibid., book 13, 2, p. 176.

26. Lu, 5–6.

27. Yu-Kung Kao, "Lyric Vision in Chinese Narrative: A Reading of Hung-lou Meng and Ju-lin Wai-shih," in *Chinese Narrative: Critical and Theoretical Essays*, ed. Andrew H. Plaks (Princeton, N.J.: Princeton University Press, 1977), 232.

28. Ibid., 228.

29. Ibid., 231.

30. Ibid., 230.

31. For example, see C. S. Song, *The Tears of Lady Meng: A Parable of People's Political Theology* (Geneva: World Council of Churches, 1981).

32. David Buttrick, *Homiletic: Moves and Structures* (Philadelphia: Fortress, 1987), 183.

33. Ibid., 179–83.

34. Lucy A. Rose, *Sharing the Word: Preaching in the Roundtable Church* (Louisville: Westminster/John Knox, 1997), 90.

35. Ludwig Wittgenstein, *Tractatus Logico-Philosophicus*, trans. C. K. Ogden (London: Kegan Paul, 1922), 27, 189, quoted from John Macquarrie, *God-Talk: An Examination of the Language and Logic of Theology* (New York: Harper & Row, 1967), 17, 24.

36. J. Rogers and D. McKim, *The Authority and Interpretation of the Bible: An Historical Approach* (San Francisco: Harper & Row, 1979), 9.

37. Ibid., 99.

38. John Calvin, *Institutes of the Christian Religion*, trans. Ford Lewis Battles (Philadelphia: Westminster, 1987), 3.2.33.

39. Donald K. McKim, "The Gospel as Empowered Speech for Proclamation and Persuasion," in *Preaching As a Theological Task*, eds. Thomas G. Long and Edward Farley (Louisville: Westminster/John Knox, 1996), 125.

40. Charles Campbell, *Preaching Jesus: New Directions for Homiletics in Hans Frei's Postliberal Theology* (Grand Rapids, Mich.: Eerdmans, 1997), 236.

41. Thomas Troeger, "A Poetics of the Pulpit for Post-Modern Times," in *Intersections: Post-Critical Studies in Preaching*, ed. Richard L. Eslinger (Grand Rapids, Mich.: Eerdmans, 1994), 47.

42. Buttrick, 116, 118–19.

43. Robert E. C. Browne, *The Ministry of the Word* (Philadelphia: Fortress, 1976), 115.

44. Ibid.

45. Ted Peters, *God — The World's Future* (Minneapolis: Fortress, 1992), 14.

46. L. Susan Bond, "Apocalyptic Vocation and Liberation: The Foolish Church in the World," in *Preaching As a Theological Task*, eds. Thomas G. Long and Edward Farley (Louisville: Westminster/John Knox, 1996), 162.

47. The term *homily*, which is rooted in Greek *homilia*, also means an "informal, popular, familiarly conversational" style of preaching in a liturgical context. See *Concise Encyclopedia of Preaching*, ed. William H. Willimon and Richard Lischer (Louisville: Westminster/John Knox, 1995), 258.

48. Cicero *De Officiis* 1.132, quoted from Robert W. Cape Jr., "Roman Women in Rhetoric and Oratory," in *Listening to Their Voices*, ed. Molly Meijer Wertheimer (Columbia: University of South Carolina Press, 1997), 117.

49. Ibid., 117–18.

50. Jane Donawerth, "Textbooks for New Audiences: Women's Revisions of Rhetorical Theory at the Turn of the Century," in *Listening to Their Voices*, ed. Molly Meijer Wertheimer (Columbia: University of South Carolina Press, 1997), 337–56.

51. Rebecca Burke, "Gertrude Buck's Rhetorical Theory," in *Occasional Papers in the History and Theory of Composition I*, ed. Donald C. Stewart (Manhattan: Kansas State University, 1978), quoted from Donawerth, 341.

52. Donawerth, 349.

53. Ibid., 348.

54. Ibid., 349.

55. Buttrick, 189.

56. Campbell, 237.

57. Ro, 106.

58. Ronald J. Allen, Barbara S. Blaisdell, and Scott Black Johnston, *Theology for Preaching* (Nashville: Abingdon, 1997), 182.

59. Rose, 108.

60. Buttrick, 188.

61. Thomas G. Long, *The Witness of Preaching* (Louisville: Westminster/John Knox, 1989), 175.

62. Rachel Blau DuPlessis, *Writing Beyond the Ending: Narrative Strategies of Twentieth-Century Women Writers* (Bloomington: Indiana University Press, 1985), 62, 239, quoted from Donawerth, 349.

Chapter Six

From Theory to Practice

Discussions in the earlier chapters about Asian American preaching articulate a set of strategies for an Asian American homiletic. Its theological foundation is God's eschatological promise in Christ Jesus for the new heaven and new earth. Its primary concern is to provide a direction for the congregation's spiritual journey.

Preparing for spiritual preaching to the Asian American congregation is like the process of preparing a meal for a family dinner. In order to cook healthy spiritual food for the congregation, the preacher uses the biblical text as a main ingredient and the congregation's distinctive cultural elements as tasty sauce. In spiritual preaching, the biblical text generates new meaning in a particular situation of the congregation through meditative spiritual hermeneutics. In the process of spiritual hermeneutics, the text functions as metaphor through which the reality of the listeners is reinterpreted to give spiritual guidance to the community of faith.

The sermon form for spiritual preaching is concerned with how effectively it accommodates the listening process of the congregation who are embedded in their particular ethnic and cultural ethos. While diverse sermonic forms proposed by contemporary homileticians are helpful for spiritual preaching, the characteristics of Asian communication suggest using a spiral-form sermon to achieve indirect communication.

Spiritual preaching also takes seriously the use of language. Realizing the limitations of human language, it understands the preaching ministry to be a co-effort by the human and the divine. God's accommodation to our limited language assures our preaching about the gospel; our ordinary language becomes the medium of divine revelation by means of the intercession of the Holy Spirit. Dialogue

151

between Asian and Western rhetoric reminds us that just as religious discourse is private conversation, so the language of preaching should be conversational. The language of conversation opens listeners to the possibility of experiencing the presence of God.

The Asian American homiletic, including such categories as the theology of preaching, biblical interpretation, sermonic form, and language, is applied to the sermon below. This sermon was preached on a Thanksgiving Sunday at the Korean Sarang Church of Princeton, New Jersey. After the service, the members were going to have a Thanksgiving banquet in the fellowship room, as most Korean American congregations did on that day. The congregation is a group of first-generation immigrants who have lived in the United States for more than twenty years on the average. Most of them have successfully overcome their hardships in the strange new land of America and have achieved economic and social stability.

The text is Deuteronomy 26:1–11, chosen from *The Common Lectionary:*

> When you have come into the land that the Lord your God is giving you as an inheritance to possess, and you possess it, and settle in it, you shall take some of the first of all the fruit of the ground, which you harvest from the land that the Lord your God is giving you, and you shall put it in a basket and go to the place that the Lord your God will choose as a dwelling for his name. You shall go to the priest who is in office at that time, and say to him, "Today I declare to the Lord your God that I have come into the land that the Lord swore to our ancestors to give us." When the priest takes the basket from your hand and sets it down before the altar of the Lord your God, you shall make this response before the Lord your God: "A wandering Aramean was my ancestor; he went down into Egypt and lived there as an alien, few in number, and there he became a great nation, mighty and populous. When the Egyptians treated us harshly and afflicted us, by imposing hard labor on us, we cried to the Lord, the God of our ancestors; the Lord heard our voice and saw our affliction, our toil, and our oppression. The Lord brought us out of Egypt with a mighty hand and an outstretched arm, with a terrifying display of power, and with signs and wonders; and he brought us into this place and gave us this land, a land flowing with milk and honey. So now I bring the first of the fruit of the ground that you, O Lord, have given me." You shall set it down before the Lord your God and bow down before the Lord your God. Then you, together with the Levites and the aliens who reside among you, shall celebrate with all the bounty that the Lord your God has given to you and to your house.

In the sermon, the text functions as metaphor to re-present the reality of the listeners. The gap between the text and the listeners is overcome by means of analogical interpretation so that the biblical story becomes the listeners' communal story. The sermon aims to describe the present situation of the congregation who are gathering for the annual Thanksgiving service from the perspective of the biblical text, rather than explaining what the text meant in the historical context or analyzing its theological concept.

The Thanksgiving service itself is the fulfillment of the meaning of the text because the text instructs a thanksgiving ceremony. The recital of memory in the text is now a confession of faith by the congregation, who can identify with the Hebrew people in the text because of their respective suffering and hardship. The communal prayer of thanksgiving in the text is now the congregation's prayer, as they thank God for deliverance and guidance; the concern for marginal people is now the commandment given to the congregation, which is called to join the same pilgrimage that the people in the text traveled. Through this metaphorical and analogical interpretation, the text functions as a lens through which the preacher and the listeners reflect on their communal and personal experiences and identify themselves with those in the Bible who took a previous journey under the guidance of God.

The structure of the text, which consists of memory, present profession, and future promise, suggests the form of the sermon. Based on this time movement, the sermonic form is designed as a spiral with five rounds. In the first round, the American Pilgrim history is told as common ground for the identity of immigrants in the United States. The second round narrows the focus on the particular experience of the congregation by recalling Korean American immigrant history as their story. The third round interprets the present situation of the congregation and describes who they are in relation to the celebration of Thanksgiving. The fourth round reminds the listeners of their responsibility as brothers and sisters to other ethnic immigrant groups as well as new Korean immigrants. Last, the sermon invites the congregation to a prayer that yearns for the fulfillment of God's eschatological promise in the world and renews their spirituality through that prayer.

The sermon engages the listeners in conversation through simple and poetic language. Rhythmic repetition, pictorial expression, and compact and crisp words invite the listeners to an active dialogue with the text, with the preacher, and with God. With a mood of unity and harmony created, they finally are led to experience the presence of God in the midst of their lives.

Sermon: Thanksgiving
Deuteronomy 26:1–11

Stuffed turkeys,
corn,
potatoes,
and freshly baked bread...
All are placed on a board set over barrels
and covered with precious linens.
Children are giggling and jumping around the table.
Finally,
a group of neighbor Indians arrive with many deer and turkeys as
    gifts.
It's time to celebrate!
The terrible winter is over!
The suffering is past!

This thanksgiving table was an expression
of the English Pilgrims' gratitude to God.
They,
aboard the *Mayflower*,
had set sail for the new continent with courage and trust in God,
and anchored on Plymouth Harbor beach in December 1620.

In the beginning, the land was cruel to these townspeople.
They knew little about hunting and fishing.
Hunger followed bitter cold winter,
disease followed hunger,
and death followed disease.

Before the spring came,
almost half of them had died.
However,
no one asked to return to their homeland,
but dared to stay in the new land
believing that this land was given to them by God.

God did not overlook their suffering.
God heard their cry
and saw their tears
and took action.

With the help of the nearby Native Americans,
they could finally harvest the firstfruits of the earth.
This land of death became a land flowing with milk and honey,
the promised land of God.

———

About three hundred years later,
across the Pacific Ocean,
there were one hundred and one people who got on an American
    merchant ship
heading toward Honolulu harbor, Hawaii.

They were Korean Christians newly converted by American
    missionaries. They started their journey
of pilgrimage
searching for God's promised land.

Arriving in January 1903 as laborers in the sugar and pineapple
    plantations, they became the first Korean settlers in America.
As soon as they landed in the new land,
they built a church where they could worship God.

Their hardship in this new land
was no less than that of the English Pilgrims.
They suffered *not* from cold weather but from cold manners,
brutal racial discrimination, and violent prejudice.

However,
they believed that this land was God's promised land
given to them and their children
as well as to the former European settlers and their offspring.

The faithful conviction and adventurous courage
of the first Korean pilgrims
became our spiritual foundation.

———

Today,
we are gathered around the altar
decorated with the new fruits of this season
to express our gratitude to God.

Turkeys,
pumpkin pies,
cooked vegetables,
and cranberry sauce...
All are set on the table.

The people around the table are
not the English Pilgrims
but we, the people of Korean Sarang Church in Princeton.

This Thanksgiving table might be unfamiliar to some of us
who have celebrated Thanksgiving in Korea
with rice cakes (*songpyen*), new crops of chestnuts, pears, and
    persimmons.

By sharing this table with one another,
we remember who we are.

Historically,
we are the heirs of the Pilgrims who landed at Plymouth Rock.
We are a part of American immigrant history.

Ethnically,
we are the heirs of the first Korean settlers.

We are proud of our distinctive cultural ethos and tradition.
We are in every way Korean
as much as we love the taste of *kimchi*.

And, above all, spiritually,
we are the heirs of Jacob
who trusted in God's promise of the land.
We are pilgrims who continue to struggle
until the day when all people belong to the promised land of God.

We remember
how hard it was to possess this new land as God's promised land.
Some of us crossed the Pacific Ocean
with little children and old parents,
with less than one hundred dollars in our pockets because of Korean
      law.
Some of us arrived at J. F. Kennedy Airport
with an uncertain future,
holding an admission letter from an American school.

All of us have struggled extremely hard
to survive in this new land
under the stress of language barriers and homesickness.
Our education and experience in Korea had little credit here.
So, many of us started as street vendors
or with less than minimum paying jobs.
Our children also suffered
from culture shock and loneliness at home alone.

But, now,
by the grace of God,
most of our church members have secure jobs
and comfortable homes
where we can relax and enjoy family life.
Our children are prospering
with the benefits of this society.

The terrible winter is over!
The suffering is past!

———

However,
we also remember those
who are still strangers on this American soil.

The Native Americans taught the Pilgrims
how to plant corn
and showed them where turkeys and ducks dwelled.
But now it's our turn.
We,
who belong to this promised land,
are to help the newcomers.

We're pilgrims called by God
to continue struggling
until the day when all immigrant people,
not only Koreans but also other ethnic groups,
fully belong to this new land
and equally inherit this promised land of God.

———

At this altar,
we pray in one voice,
"Thank you, Lord, for giving us our daily bread.
May your kingdom come
and your will
be done in this land. Amen."

Index